BEYOND TIME

Ideas of the Great Philosophers
on
Eternal Existence and Immortality

Charles J. Caes

UNIVERSITY
PRESS OF
AMERICA

LANHAM • NEW YORK • LONDON

Copyright © 1985 by

University Press of America,® Inc.

4720 Boston Way
Lanham, MD 20706

3 Henrietta Street
London WC2E 8LU England

Library of Congress Cataloging in Publication Data

Caes, Charles J.
  Beyond time.

  Bibliography: p.
  Includes index.
  1. Eternity—History of doctrines.   2. Future
life—History of doctrines.   3. Immortality—History
of doctrines.   I. Title.
BT912.C34   1985   129   85-17864
ISBN 0-8191-4933-0 (alk. paper)
ISBN 0-8191-4934-9 (pbk. : alk. paper)

to
Nettie M. Rigg
and in memory of
William K. Rigg (1906-1975)

CONTENTS

INTRODUCTION

This book is designed as a survey of classical ideas on eternity and immortality and as an introduction to the works of some of the great philosophers, men such as Kant, Aquinas, Augustine, Aristotle. It is not intended to be a complete history of all the philosophy on these two subjects but a collection of the foremost writings and ideas not ordinarily available to the reader unless he or she has the time to consult many separate volumes of materials.

The text which follows may be divided into three parts. The first would consist of chapters one through four and would be concerned with the subject of eternity, the necessity of God's eternalness and the possibility of the soul's, and the probability of a state which exists "between" time and eternity. The second would consist of the chapters five through eight and would be concerned with immortality and the purpose and value of life. The third would be chapters nine and ten, which are a summary of the religious arguments and of the ideas on eternity and immortality.

In approaching these subjects, the book follows this track: unless there does indeed exist a state in which things know eternal existence, immortality is out of the question. Yet, the fact that there is such a thing as eternity does not guarantee individual immortality.

Throughout the first eight chapters, religious arguments for either eternity or immortality are ignored, for this is a book on the philosophy of eternity and immortality, not a book on religious beliefs. However, a summary of religious beliefs is given in the ninth chapter. Philosophy is concerned with an investigation of the facts and principles of reality. Religion is mainly a means of worshipping God; it is founded on faith. This does not mean that religion is without philosophy, only that its philosophy is based on premises which themselves have not been proven by philosophical investigation. This may read at first as a slight against religion but it is not meant to be; consider, if you will, that experience shows that to each new plateau of awareness that philosophy brings us, ideal faith seems to have already brought others there.

The question of eternity is not one on which philosophers have generally cared to spend much time. They treat it, generally, as an aside in their investigations of the existence of God, of His attributes, and in their investigations of other subjects such as the soul itself and its immortality. The question of the soul, or the individual, and its afterlife, however, has always been a primary concern of philosophy.

Why should it be? Beside the personal hope of continued

existence that would drive one to search for the proof, knowledge of immortality is certainly a knowledge that would modify one's behavior. Consider simply, if you will, the development of a moral philosophy, personal or general. It is not only important to society but it gives direction to the individual man or woman. It is no novel or daring observation that any philosophy constructed from atheism would undergo extreme revision once the existence of God is proven. Some may counter that it is indeed possible that an atheistic philosophy can be drawn with the highest good in mind, but *highest good* and God are synonymous terms, and any atheist dedicating his life to the highest good is an atheist in name only, not in practice.

The idea of, or hope of, immortality must be important to a man or woman's mental perspective and emotional balance. For one, it helps that individual deal with the fact of their own individual worth in the universe of things. The earth alone, with its great mountains, its great bodies of water, dwarfs or drowns every individual's image of himself. The endless sky and the galaxies of stars and planets make every individual feel even more minute. Yet he and she knows that they are in possession of very special qualities that set them apart from other things in the universe. It is individuality and will. It makes little sense to an individual that one day he or she will cease to exist. Yet he or she witnesses death, learns of death, and sees no proof of immortality beyond what a few teleological observations might offer. If an individual accepts his or her existence as being temporary, survival becomes the primary preoccupation of life. But if one accepts that there is an eternity ahead, then intellectual growth and spiritual development become the order. And who would argue that this last perspective would not lead one to a lifestyle far and above that which would be conducted by someone assuming only a temporal existence.

This century has seen science and medicine combine forces to create a wave of skepticism that can crush the deistic views of any individual who has not developed a strong philosophical basis for his religious behavior. Now, that may sound contradictory because religion is faith-based, but one must remember that even the great patrons of the Church, Anselm and Aquinas among them, saw the need to develop philosophical arguments. Faith, of course, came first to them but they sensed the need for a philosophical "rock" on which to build or defend that faith.

Additionally, this era of great advances in science and the medical arts, this era of preoccupation with physical necessity that could lead us all to be slaves to our own technology and desires, this world of machines and "natural" science leaves little oxygen for the more noble ideas and concerns of the great religions of the world, these ideas which transcend the merely natural concerns of sensual pleasure and life-extension.

Everyone is, in his or her own right, a philosopher. But how selfish or sophisticated that philosophy may be will depend, for the most part, upon the individual's feelings, experiences, impressions — what works for them. In many cases one's philosophy is after-the-fact. That is, rather than to be living by a prescribed philosophy people develop a philosophy based on the way they live, what suits their way of life. Rarely do they stop to consider philosophy on strictly formal terms. Little, if anything at all, do they know about Kant, Leibnitz, Aquinas, Boethius, Aristotle. Little are they sure, even, of God.

But this book is presented with the modest objectives of introducing great ideas, not in converting anyone. It is designed to introduce the answers or arguments put forth by great philosophers of the past concerning the subjects of God, eternity, immortality, good and evil. The relative value of these insights or speculations is left to the reader to judge.

CHAPTER 1
Concepts of Eternity

Any starbright night when the evening sky seems lit for some universal celebration, treat yourself to this dazzling view of thousands of incredibly hot luminous globular masses appearing as tiny dots of light. In actuality, of course, they are as large as, or larger than, the sun which heats our planet. And bear in mind that what you are actually seeing represents only a small percentage of the stars that may actually exist. After all, the human eye is a highly limited mechanism and its reach into the grand splendor of our galaxy is minimal.

Scientists assign these stars into "levels of magnitude" according to their visibility. The brightest stars are assigned a *zero* magnitude — except for the three very, very brightest stars which, for purposes of relative comparison, are assigned a negative magnitude. These three stars — Sirius, Canopius and Arcturus — are easily visible to the naked eye, that is the eye not dressed with telescope or binoculars. And also visible to the unassisted eye are all the stars which display in zero magnitude. With help from the great lenses which bring the world of the astronomer a bit closer for investigation, you and I can see stars even of the 6th magnitude. But even if we have in view, all at one time, stars of the first six magnitudes, we have in sight only a small sample of the stellar population.

True it is that even with the most advanced telescopes we see only a small portion of the stars that, in all probability, exist. The universe is so extraordinary that it may indeed be infinite. The number of stars may be endless — endless! There is no way to know for sure.

Consider what we now know of the organization of that part of the universe with which we are familiar, beginning with the one planet on which we know life exists, but which an elementary knowledge of probability lets us assume cannot be the only system with some type of organic form. This planet, of course, is Earth, a member of the humble solar system consisting of the Sun, a few planets and other celestial forms such as comets and meteors. This solar system is only one of many and it inhabits a galaxy, named the Milky Way, consisting of about 100 billion stars. To travel the diameter of the Milky Way would cost a man or a woman 100,000 light years of their lives. As the life span of a man or a woman is too instantaneous to even be measured in terms of light years, there is no possibility of any individual even considering a star-hopping tour around the galaxy. But should someone find his way to a solar system pinching the rim of the Milky Way System he would only find that there are just as many worlds above him as below him (if we can use those terms in relation to space), that beyond this galaxy there are others, and these also possibly containing a hundred billion stars each.

If space is infinite, the number of galaxies may well be infinite, and, therefore stars and their solar systems, too.

To say that something is infinite is to say that it has no limit, that it extends beyond all measure. Is it really possible that anything at all can be infinite? After all, our lives, our world and almost everything with which we work or conduct our investigations is found to be limited except, perhaps, in the area of mathematics. Here we are quite use to using the term and understanding that it truly exists. After all, we know that if we were to live forever we could go on counting forever. There is no last number nor can we conceive of a final positional notation beyond which we could not represent the next number. Thus, in mathematics we tend to do an about-face. Here we find it quite conceivable that negative or positive possibilities are infinite, without limit. Yet, if we look into the sky we cannot imagine infiniteness. As vast as the heavens may be they must have a limit. Yet, where does the universe end or who has proof that it does indeed?

If we consider the concept which the term *infinite* forces into our minds we envision something which is boundless in either direction, that is, in terms of minimums and maximums. That is, that it goes forward forever and backward forever. It is actually forever before and forever after. If it is truly infinite it is boundless in terms of extension, whether we attempt to trace its point of ending or its point of beginning. It has no alpha as well as no omega. It is like a circle. You may define points in its circumference and evaluate it in geometric terms. You may find a symbol by which you represent it and arbitrarily strike a point on the symbol and say that you will measure from here to there and fix arbitrarily any reference point as its beginning. But there is, of course, no way for you to define where the circle begins and where it ends. Physically, of course, you may infer that it had to have begun at some point but then that is to infer that it was something else before it became a circle; but *conceptually,* a circle is a circle.

Forever before and *forever* after! Infinite.

Now, when we think of the word *forever* and what it actually implies, we realize that "before" and "after" become redundant. *Forever* simply implies something which *is* at all times. Past and future. It is *always.*

Then, when we think of the term *always,* we begin to realize what we mean when we refer to someone or something as being eternal, what we mean when we refer to a condition or a state as eternity.

II

Often, the words *eternal* and *immortal* are used interchangeably, though they should not be. To put it simply, that which is immortal will continue forever but it had a beginning; that which is eternal will also continue forever but it has had no beginning, for it existed always. Thus, one thinks of man as possibly being immortal but thinks of God as being eternal.

The idea of eternity has been a subject that has preoccupied mankind for thousands of years. It might well be listed along with the existence of God, freedom and immortality as one of the special objectives for speculative investigation. Some may find fault with such an assumption but if they consider for a moment that man has generally considered eternalness as a necessary attribute of God, if there is no such thing as eternity, man's general concept of God needs to be given extensive revision.

Additionally, it has always been difficult for men and women to accept the idea of their own eventual corruption and non-existence and they have always sought to find some connection with a supernatural order guaranteeing immortality. As things which are eternal cannot be totally corrupted, though they may indeed change form, if there is at least this thing called eternalness, and it is an attritube of the Creator, then there is sufficient argument for the immortality of men and women.

The word eternity has three main interpretations. In the one case, it is the concept of time as being forever before and forever after; it is seen as an unending extent of time in either direction. In the second case, eternity and time are two completely different notions altogether. In the third case, eternity is a state which includes time but yet precedes and excludes it.

It is the first definition which most people use when speaking about the idea matter-of-factly. However, in philosophy it is probably more common to find the second definition, which sees eternity as separate from time, being used.

One can easily get caught up in arguing for the one definition or the other. But whether eternity is simply timelessness or a state containing but preceding and continuing after time, the idea of anything at all having always been, and being forever, is quite a test for any intellect.

When one, however, begins to contemplate the matter of a source for all existence, he quickly realizes that, in the final analysis, there are only two possibilities: at one time something suddenly appeared from nothing at all or there is something, or someone, which has always existed.

Of the two possibilities, the sudden appearance of something from nothing is the least plausible. We have yet to experience in our world of sensations anything at all which has come from nothing. This, however, does not make the idea of an eternal something, or especially of an eternal *someone,* any easier to grasp — for we have never been able to find any substance or develop any formidable proof that anything at all anywhere in the universe has always been.

Perhaps, if we (meaning you and I) turn first to St. Thomas Aquinas we can begin an investigation into the subject and proceed to look at some of the great ideas about eternity which famous philosophers and theologians have developed for us.

Aquinas uses the term and discusses the concept throughout his *Summa Theologica.* He begins to introduce us, though it was not his primary intention, to the idea of eternity during one of his arguments for the existence of God.

He explains[1] that in our world of physical things there is a series of efficient causes. He quite rightly indicates that there is no known case, or even any possibility, of there being something in our universe which caused itself; if it could cause itself then it must have been prior to itself, and that is clearly not possible. Somewhere, sometime, somehow, he infers, there must have been something, therefore, which was the cause of itself.

"Now in efficient causes," Aquinas writes, "it is not possible to go on to infinity, because in all efficient causes following in order, the first is the cause of the intermediate cause, and the intermediate is the cause of the ultimate cause, whether the intermediate cause be several, or one only. Now to take away the cause is to take away the effect. Therefore, if there be no first cause among efficient causes, there will be no ultimate, nor any intermediate cause. But if in efficient causes it is possible to go to infinity, there will be no first efficient cause, neither will there be an ultimate effect, nor any intermediate efficient causes, all of which is plainly false. Therefore it is necessary to admit a first efficient cause, to which everyone gives the name of God."[2]

Many will argue that the first efficient cause need not be that which we call God but can be anything at all from a chemical formula to a gaseous substance; but whatever that first efficient cause is, it has the unique attribute of eternalness. Aquinas, in his third way of proving the existence of God, states this. " . . . . . We find in nature things that are possible to be and not to be, since they are found to be generated, and to be corrupted and consequently they are possible to be and not to be. But it is impossible for these always to exist, for that which is possible not to be at sometime is not. Therefore if everything is possible not to be, then at one time there could have been nothing in existence, because that which does exist only begins to exist by something already existing." He goes on to stress that if there were anytime in the past in which nothing existed there would be no possible way for something to suddenly come into existence. If there was nothing from which it could come, or any matter at all from which it could be formed, how could it come into existence? Thus, if there were ever, at anytime, a period, no matter how slight, in which nothing at all existed, this state of non-existence would have to continue to even today. Thus, he concludes that there must be something which has a necessary existence. We have little choice but to admit the existence of "some being having of itself its own necessity, and not receiving it from another, but rather causing in others their neces- sity . . . . ."[3] One might readily argue that this necessary existence need not be a being, but then how could we account for the intelligence found in beings throughout the world.

Aquinas offers to explain the incredible state in which this being exists in his chapter on the eternity of God. He writes as follows:[4]

" . . . As we attain to the knowledge of simple things by way of compound things, so we must reach the knowledge of eternity by means of time, which is nothing but "the numbering of movement by before and after."[5] Since succession occurs in every movement, and one part must necessarily follow another, the fact that we can recognize before and after in movement gives us the ability to understand time, which is nothing else but the measure of before and after in movement. Now when anything lacks movement and always exists in the same state, it is impossible to measure time, for, in this case, there is no before and no after. "And as therefore the nature of time consists in the numbering of before and after in movement, so

5

likewise in the apprehension of the uniformity of what is altogether outside of movement consists the nature of eternity."

He further explains that those things which are determined to be measured by time will also be generated and corrupted in time; they will have their beginning and ending in time, "as is said in the *Physics,** because in everything which is moved there is a beginning and there is an end. But as whatever is wholly immutable can have no succession, so it has no beginning, and no end. Thus eternity is known from two sources: first, because what is eternal is immutable —that is, lacks beginning and end (that is, no term either way); secondly, because eternity lacks succession being simultaneously whole."

Aquinas distinguishes eternity from time, but not because eternity lacks a beginning and an end, for this, he claims, is simply an accidental difference. The real reason eternity is different from time is because eternity is the measure of a permanent being and therefore simultaneously whole whereas time is simply a measure of movement.

To Aquinas, then, eternity can be marked by its having no term whatever and, therefore, having no beginning, no end and no such thing as succession. His ideas, however, though formulated more than 700 years ago, were not new. He did, in fact, borrow some of his ideas from a Roman philosopher who wrote in the 6th Century A.D. Aquinas mentions him by name in Article 4, Question 10 of the first part of *Summa*. This earlier philosopher was a man by the name of Anicius Manlius Servinus Boethius, and that work of his from which Aquinas drew was titled *De Consolitione Philosphiae*, which, translated, is *The Consolation of Philosophy*.

Boethius (480-524) was a well-to-do Roman, also well-educated, and a student of the works of both Plato and Aristotle. By the time he had reached the age of 30 he had become a consul and not too long afterward became the principal minister to Theodoric the Ostrogoth who ruled Italy from 493 to 536. Despite the burdens of his official office, Boethius continued to pour out works on mathematics, music, Christianity and philosophy. But during his political career he made enough enemies to be framed for treason, for which he was tried and convicted, exiled, imprisoned and then executed (524).

It was while he was in prison that he penned *De Consolitione Philosophiae*, which is considered his masterpiece.

To Boethius, eternity is the total possession of infinite life all at once. It is the here and now because it has no past and no future. This

*He is referring to Aristotle's work.

is a rather exhausting concept for the casual reader to grasp, but the idea becomes much clearer when we compare eternity with those things which exist in time. In Book 5 (of *Consolation*) he writes that all that lives in time, under its conditions, is in constant movement from the past to the present to the future; anything which lives in time can not possibly have the ability to grasp all at one time the entire space of its lifetime. Whatever has come before it is lost and it has no ability to know what waits in tomorrow. "And in this life of today your life is no more than a changing, passing moment. And as Aristotle said of the universe so it is of all that is subject to time; though it never began to be, nor will ever cease, and its life is coexistent with the infinity of time, yet it is not such as can be held to be eternal. For though it apprehends and grasps a space of infinite lifetime; it has not yet grasped the future. What we should rightly call eternal is that which grasps and possesses wholly and simultaneously the fullness of unending life, which lacks naught of the future, and has lost naught of the fleeting past; and such an existence must be ever present in itself to control and aid itself, and also must keep present with itself the infinity of changing time . . . . . "

Boethius goes on to say that those who imagine that the universe is coeternal with God, because it had no beginning and can have no end, are under a grave misconception. Passing through unending life is an entirely different thing than grasping the entire infiniteness of unending life in the present. Boethius states that such ability is a property peculiar only to the mind of God.

Moving further back into history, to hundreds of years before Boethius, we come upon another noted philosopher who also distinguished eternity from time. His name is Plotinus (205-270); he was an Egyptian philosopher who spent the greater part of his life as a student and did not actually begin his writings until he was nearly fifty years old. At age 28 he became the disciple of a respected teacher and philospher named Ammonius and remained with him for about eleven years, after which time he embarked on a series of travels with the intention of studying Persian and Indian philosophies. But the year 245 A.D., however, found him in Rome — as a teacher now instead of student. His subject: philosophy.

Plotinus had little use for this life and he was a man who had little care about material things. He envisioned death as an opportunity to be free from the confines of the physical world. As the writings which he left behind each contained within them nine treatises, they have come to be known as the Enneads.

7

In the *First Ennead* (5th Tractate), Plotinus writes of time as being nothing more than a mimic of eternity. He argues that "whatever it is that time would absorb and seal to itself of that which remains permanent in eternity, will eventually be annihilated in its temporal state, saved otherwise only because in some degree it still belongs to eternity. However, it will be totally destroyed if it is unconditionally absorbed into the state of temporal things."

Plotinus continues to say that if happiness requires experience of the good life, it has little to do with the life of worldly pleasures, but, has instead, to do with the life of Authentic-Existence. The life of Authentic-Existence cannot be measured as we measure things of a temporal nature for the Authentic-Existence of which he speaks is eternal in nature. "And eternity is not a more or a less thing of any magnitude but is the unchangeable, the indivisible, is timeless Being."

To this he adds, "We must not muddle together Being and Non-Being, time and eternity, not even everlasting time with the eternal; we cannot make lapses and stages of an absolute unity; all must be taken together, wheresoever and howsoever we handle it; and it must be taken at that, not even as an undivided block of time but as the Life of Eternity, a stretch not made up of periods but completely rounded, outside of all notion of time."

In the 7th Tractate of the *Third Ennead,* Plotinus again emphasizes that eternity and time are two completely different things, eternity having its existence in what he calls the *everlasting kind* and time having its existence only through possession and only in the universe that we understand. He writes that eternity requires something essentially complete though it is without sequence. " . . . a close enough definition of eternity would be that it is a life limitless in the full sense of being all the life there is and a life which, knowing nothing of past or future to shatter its completeness, possesses itself intact forever. To the notion of a Life (a Living Principle) all-comprehensive add that it never spends itself, and we have the statement of a life instantaneously infinite.

" . . . the conception of Eternity demands something which is in its nature compelte without sequence; it is not satisfied by something measured out to any remoter time or even by something limitless, but, in its limitless reach, still having the progression of futurity: it requires something immediately possessed of the due fullness of Being, something whose Being does not depend upon any quantity (such as instalments of time) but subsists before all quantity." ·

Leaving Plotinus and his ideas now and stepping even further back into history we come to Aristotle (384-322 B.C.), who considered whether those things which are eternal in nature consist of elements. If they did, he indicates, they would have to contain matter for anything that is made of elements is composite. But if something requires any series of elements in order for it to exist, then it is capable of not existing. Thus, these things which are composite cannot be eternal by definition. It follows, then, according to Aristotle, that anything which is eternal cannot consist of elements. "No substance," he writes, "has the attribute of eternalness unless it is in its essence actuality. That which is imperishable, and therefore eternal, exists actually."[6]

Of whatever it is that the eternal consists, then, this thing (for want of a better word) is not divisible, for it does not consist of matter. That which we may define, or suppose, is eternal then must not be material in nature. Should there be a God, He cannot be a material substance but of a form very alien to ours.

Plato (428 B.C. - 348 B.C.) also considered the subject of eternity; but Plato was a philosopher who did not always deal with his subject matter on strictly scholastic terms. Often he preferred to deal with topics such as *creation* or *soul* on highly creative levels, constructing stories based more on possibility than probability and developed with the sole intention of exciting the mind of the reader or listener than in actually presenting full-proof arguments. This does not mean, however, that his stories possessed no wisdom or were without satisfactory ideas.

Take, for instance, his *Timaeus*,[7] in which he tells the story of the creation and attempts to guess at God's motivation. It is, of course, purely a tale, and Plato does not expect it to be taken as anything but a tale; however, the reasoning and ideas that are presented in it Plato would have expected to be taken seriously and indeed they have been.

According to Plato, when God created the universe, His first desire was to make it as perfectly as He could and *that which is perfect must be eternal,* for not to possess eternalness would be to lack something, and to be in need of something is a sign of imperfection.

As Plato describes it, God also desired that men and women be everlasting but this was, apparently, an impossibility. So he decided to solve this dilemma by making an image of eternity; this image, however, possessing motion. Thus, when He made the heavens, He made them eternal, but moving according to number, and this movement man defines as time.

9

Plato goes on to indicate that before the heavens were created, there were no days, no nights, no months, no years. When God created the heavens, however, he also created these events from which we construct our calendars.

Days and nights, months and years, Plato explains, are all parts of time and the past and the future are simply what he calls created species of time, and these we mistakenly include as a part of the eternal essence.

"We say *He was, He will be,* Plato explains, "but the only real truth is that *is* alone is properly attributed to Him and the words *was* and *will be* are only to be spoken of becoming in time, for they are motions. But that which is immovable, always the same, cannot become older or younger for these are occurrences which only take place in time. God can never be older or younger, nor is he subject at all to any of these states which affect motion and sensible things, and of which generation is the cause. These are the forms of time, which *imitates eternity* and revolves according to a law of number . . . . "[8]

Plato believed that time and the universe came into existence at exactly the same instant, if only because having been crated together they might one day be terminated together. But when both the universe and time come to their end, there will still be those things which partake of eternity.

Thus we can see, generally, how his ideas on eternity and time were shaped for Aquinas, who is perhaps the most influential philosopher and theologian of all time, by writers and teachers such as Boethius, Plotinus, Aristotle and Plato. These men saw time and eternity as two completely different states of existence, time being the state of corruptable things with a past, present and future, but eternity being an ever present state of everlasting and permanent quality.

III

Turning abruptly now from ancient times to the 16th Century, we come across the writings of Michel De Montaigne (1533-1592), the French philosopher and essayist. In his *Essais*[9] where he discusses *being* and man's inability to comprehend it, he offers his definition of the eternal which he says "never had a beginning nor shall have an ending." He maintains that that which is eternal is immutable. Time, on the other hand, he adds, is a mobile thing that is forever on the move, forever in the process of change. Time is no measure of eternity, for eternity precedes and follows time.

John Locke (1632-1704), the great English philosopher considered the terms *time* and *eternity* in his *Concerning Human Understanding.* He concerned himself with just how the idea of eternity came into our understanding; and how our idea of eternity is, for the most part, limited to space and duration, and so much so that one easily accepts that if there is a God, He fills all of eternity — but at the same time does not so easily grasp the idea that God fills immensity. In Chapter 14 of *Understanding,* he writes: "His finite being is certainly as boundless one way as another and I think it ascribes a little too much to matter to say that where there is no body there is nothing."

But Locke does offer direction on just how he feels one must perceive of eternity in relation to time. He does so in the last section of Chapter 15. Here he discusses duration and time and in so doing paints a picture of eternity encircling time, and God, at His eternal throne, has control of *the past, present and future all at once!* It is as though all of life has been recorded on an endless videotape to be reversed or forward-fed as the Creator may so choose to do.

"Duration, and time, which is a part of it, is the idea we have of perishing distance, of which no two parts exist together, but follow each other in succession; and expansion is the idea of lasting distance, all whose parts exist together, and are not capable of succession. And therefore, though we cannot conceive of any duration without succession, nor can put it in our thoughts that any being does not now exist tomorrow or possess at once more than the present moment of duration, yet we can conceive the eternal duration of the Almighty far different from that of any man, or any future being."

Locke explains that this is so because man cannot know all past and future things. What lies in the past for man lies there forever, never to be retrieved — at least not by him. What lies in the future lies there unti it finally occurs; man cannot reach out to it and make it a present event.

But with God, it is possible to recall the past and make present the future. "God's infinite duration, accompanied with infinite knowledge and infinite power, allows him to see all things, past and to come; and they are no more distant from his knowledge, no further removed from His sight, then the present; they all lie under the same view; and there is nothing which He cannot make exist each moment He pleases. For the existence of all things, depending upon His good pleasure, exist every moment that He thinks fit to have them exist . . . "

Immanuel Kant (1724-1804), the noted German philosopher, turned his attention briefly on the idea of eternity and the possibility of such a state. While he was not directly inerested in proving that eternity is indeed a reality he did develop further some of the ideas of Baruch Spinoza (1632-1677) and expressed that time and space as we know it is not reality in its truest sense. He falls back on his theories of conscience and the existence of a moral commander to point to the possibility of immortality. If there is the possibility of immortality then there is indeed something which transcends time. If there is a state which transcends time (though this is not the way Kant expressed it) it can very well be extended infinitely in one direction as well as another.

IV

Many philosophers have argued that there is an eternal cosmic cycle, often referred to as cyclical recurrence, which assures that universal events will occur over and over again. Just as the universe was born as the result of some unexplainable and great explosion, so, too, will it one day be brought to complete destruction — but only to be reborn again as the result of another great conflagration. This cycle of death and rebirth is said to go on forever; it can never end. And with each rebirth there must follow the same cosmic patterns that would create, just as before, the matter which *must* evolve into the galaxies of stars and planets and into living things. Additionally, the theory of cyclical recurrence holds, whatever life has existed before will exist again. Socrates, Plato, Augustine, Aquinas will live to teach and write again. The numerical order which originates with each rebirth must continue as it always has with each cosmic cycle.

Plotinus liked this idea of eternity. In his *Fifth Ennead* he considers whether or not there is an ideal archetype of individual beings. In so doing he explains that it is necessary to consider whether he and every other human being originates from the *Intellectual*, where everything has its origin and principle.

"If it is true that Socrates' soul is eternal," Plotinus writes, "then the Authentic Socrates — to adopt the term — must be there; this is to say his individual soul has its existence not only in this world but in the Supreme. If there is no such permanent endurance — and what was Socrates may with change of time become another soul and be Pythogoras or someone else — then the individual Socrates has not that existence in the Supreme."

Plotinus goes on to point out that every individual soul inherits what he calls the *Reason Principles* which are existent in the cosmos. And since the cosmos contains the reason principles of every living thing, so, too, must the soul. This being so, the soul's awareness, so to speak, must be boundless unless there is "a periodical renovation bounding the boundlessness by the return of a former series."

But if there is this periodic return, Plotinus asks, why must there exist distinct archetypes? Couldn't one archetypal man be sufficient for all, and likewise a "limited number of souls produce a limitless number of men?"

He answers his own question by explaining that no one *Reason Principle* is sufficient to represent individuals who are distinct. "One human being cannot be sufficient as the paragon for many beings distinct from each other not merely in material forms but also by countless variations of ideal types. There is no doubt that various pictures or images can reproduce the original Socrates; the beings produced differ so exceptionally as to demand distinct *Reason Principles,* and, so, too, the same existents appear once more under the action."

Plotinus imagines that there must be identical reproductions of someone from one cosmic period to another but that there cannot be identical reproduction during the same period. He writes that when the universe has completed its term, it will begin a new existence, "since the entire Quantity which the cosmos is to exhibit, every item that is to emerge in its course, all is laid up from the first in the Being that contains the Reason-Principle."

Augustine (354-430) considered this question of cosmic recurrence in his *"City of God"*[10] but he argues against the concept — more on religious than on philosophical grounds:

"Some, too, in advocating these recurring cycles that restore all things to their original cite in favor of their supposition what Solomon says in the book of Ecclesiastes: "What is that which hath been? It is that which shall be. And what is that which is done? It is that which shall be done. And there is no new thing under the sun. Who can speak and say, See, this is new? It hath been already of old time, which was before us."

Augustine explains that Solomon was referring to the generations of man, to the cycle of the heavens, to creatures which live and die. His meaning was that all that lives and that we observe has existed before us and will exist after us. And as all things exist in God eternally, everything in a sense has already been in existence even before its actual cration. Augustine ridicules the idea that Plato will return again with the next cosmic cycle to teach again in the Academy in Athens. He quotes from Scripture to reinforce that as Christ died to atone for the sins of man, and rose again, he would die no more. And he quotes again from Scripture to indicate that "we ourselves after the resurrection will be forever with the Lord."

Following Augustine's line of thought, most Christian philosophers have argued against the idea of cyclical recurrence. For one thing, it goes too strongly against the idea of each man's individuality, as well as his relationship with God, which, in Christianity, is based on a union with Christ and adherence to the will of God — all culminating in a Last Judgement. The idea of a Last Judgement alone would negate any idea of cyclical recurrence. Besides, according to Aquinas, even God does not possess the power to recreate identical individuals because that in itself is a contradiction and there is no contradiction in God.

Since Aquinas, philosophers and theologians have generally only toyed with the idea of cyclical recurrence. Men like Newton, Descartes, Spinoza and Kant — to name just a few — acknowledged a general periodic cycle in nature but they felt it was generally unwarranted to try and project that cycle to all of the created universe.

Frederick Nietzche (1844-1900), however, saw a great deal of merit in it and believed that there was unquestionable scientific truth to the idea of cyclical recurrence. He saw himself coming back time after time and, therefore, would be, as every man should be, compelled to make his life worth returning to.

In Nietzche's *The Will to Power,* we see how the idea of eternal recurrence kept revealing itself to Nietzche. In this text which is really a collection of his notes over about a six year period, we find that his preoccupation with the subject began about June 10, 1887, when he started his notes with ideas about the immortality of nature, its meaninglessness. And this very pointlessness of all that exists and all that man contrives, he sees as a comedy of sorts. And the idea of life in vain, "existence as it is, without meaning or aim, yet recurring inevitably without any finale of nothingness" is totally encompassed by the concept of eternal recurrence.[11]

V

In summary: The word eternity may have three generally accepted interpretations.

1) That of time being forever before and forever after.

2) That of a state separate altogether from time and transcending it.

3) That of a state including time but preceding and exceeding it.

The idea of anything always possessing existence and always continuing to exist is no easy one to accept. But the idea of eternity has preoccupied even the ancient Greeks.

Plato believed that time and the universe came into existence at exactly the same moment. But before time and the universe existed, that which is eternal, God, existed — God, Who lives in an eternal state and is immovable, always the same, and cannot become older or younger because such occurrences can only take place in time.

Aristotle explained that those things which exist in eternity cannot be made up of elements, for no substance has the attribute of eternalness unless it is, in its essence, actuality. That which is imperishable, and therefore eternal, exists actually.

Plotinus felt that the concept of eternity demands that it be something which is in its nature complete though without sequence. "It requires something which is immediately possessed of the fullness of being, something where being is not at all dependent on any quantity but rather subsists before all quantity."

Boethius argued that the only things that can be truly eternal are those which can contain wholly and simultaneously the entire fullness of unending life, which at one time possesses the future with the past.

To St. Thomas Aquinas, eternity can be marked by its having no term whatever, and, therefore, having no beginning, no end, and no such thing as succession.

The French essayist and philosopher, Michel De Montaigne taught that that which is eternal "never had a beginning nor shall have an ending."

John Locke envisioned eternity as the natural state of God and he wrote that it is possible for God, reigning in that state, to recall the past and make present the future. To Locke, this eternal God is capable of seeing all things and the past and the future are no more distant from his knowledge than the present.

Some philosophers have toyed with the idea of an eternal cosmic cycle, often referred to as cyclical recurrence, which assures that universal events will occur over and over again.

Plotinus argued for the idea of cyclical recurrence. Augustine dismissed it on religious grounds and Aquinas claimed that even God has not the power to create identical individuals.

The idea of cyclical recurrence was given little serious attention from Aquinas until the time of Frederick Nietzche, who was overtaken with the idea.

But so what? What difference does it make in the universal scheme of things if the common (only common in the sense that they are concerned with practical knowledge) man and woman is or is not aware of things which may have an eternal nature.

First, it would reinforce the arguments for the existence of God. This would be so because we naturally associate the attribute of eternalness with God. If what we mean by God is *our* creator Who lives in all perfection, if He does not possess eternalness, He cannot be all-perfect. And knowing — knowing in the sense of being *closer to* certainty — of the probability of God *must* affect the attitudes and ethics of each and everyone.

Secondly, if there is indeed some being who possesses eternalness — even if it is not that which we conceive of as God — there is the *possibility* (not guarantee) of eternal existence for all things. That leads to the hope for each and every man and woman that they, too, in their essence (or souls), are incorruptible and in passing from this existence will not pass into oblivion.

Therefore, while the relationship between time and eternity may not be relevant, whether or not there is such a thing as eternity would appear to be highly relevant.

CHAPTER 2
The Eternalness of God

✷ Eternity and God are concepts so closely associated that one cannot think of the one and not the other unless, of course, he or she is a confirmed atheist. From a purely philosophical perspective, there has never been a sufficient proof of the existence of God; that is, there has never been any single argument that proves *without any doubt* at all that God exists. In the very final analysis this is where the argument for atheism rests.

But, on the other hand, either is there proof that He does not exist. However, it is customary in arguments for the existence of something, that the burden of proof lie with those supporting that existence. Yet the absence of proof is never considered a conclusive argument.

The very concept of a deity, the atheists might argue, was created by early man to compensate for his fear of the unknown, to put some reason behind the things which he could not understand, to use as a means of subjugating others or in winning security in one's assumed position in society as priest or magi or prophet. After all, enough philosophers admit that man can only come upon knowledge through experience and there is no one we know of that has experienced God and can prove it. Therefore any idea of him is nothing more than that; there is nothing in reality that corresponds to this idea.

One, then, recognizes the necessity of the Christ in Christian theology as one means by which to counter the atheist; for in Jesus of Nazareth, the world had a credible witness to His existence. True it is that God transcends woman and man and their universe and there is no possible way we can experience Him completely. We may *possibly,* though not probably, experience Him, should He exist, in some material form, as a burning bush, as a voice, as a dream-like image, as even a man — but in any of these representations we experience Him only in a form taken so that we can communicate. To assume that the fire, the bush, the voice, or the man actually represents God in his entirety is absurd; these are but media for communication. Besides, who is it that is so far above others that the privilege of a personal witness should be afforded to him or her? And if he or she did indeed come upon God, as some have claimed to have done, how can they determine if they actually have? They may be frauds or individuals so caught up in religious experience that they have fooled themselves.

Thus the meaning to Christians of the one called Jesus of Nazareth, who was God Incarnate (according to *most* Christian sects), and whose pure life and extreme dedication to truth and the highest good made him a witness of unchallengeable credibility.

But to the atheist, the books of the bible are simply narratives constructed by individuals who saw the need to deify a man with whom they were obsessed and in whose life and teachings they found a model by which all future generations might benefit. And as much of what has been laid down since men and women first learned to carve or print alphamerics has been utter fraud, inaccurate or just totally incorrect, they have some strong basis for being suspicious of the written word. Atheism does not represent the self-serving perspective that many might ascribe to it; it is often the result of a response to betrayal that individual men and women have experienced by others and which they have noted from their studies in history.

Some would point the atheist to the sequence of causes and events and say here is a sign of intelligence; but still the atheist fails to find proof of an intellect being involved in the process. We live in a universe of constant motion which necessitates constant change. There will always be motion and change right up until the time our universe collapses and even beyond that time, for our universe will leave a void that will undoubtedly be refilled by other universes or by our own again when it explodes and expands into its next cycle. Motion and change the atheist sees as eternal events, universal *principles.*

William Paley (1743-1805) was one of the many philosophers who found easy argument against such perspective. In his *Natural Theology,*[1] he wrote that in tracing causes we may hever appear to come upon general properties that indicate the presence of intellect, but the very managing of these properties, the very use we see made of them, demands that we admit somewhere behind it all there is an intelligence at work. Paley gives this example: " . . . suppose animal secretions to be elective sanctions, and that such and such attractions universally belong to such and such substances, in all which there is no intellect concerned; still the chance and callocation of these substances, the fixing upon right substances, and supposing them in right places, must be an act of intelligence." He then asks us what mischief would follow if there were just the slightest transposition of the secretory organs, just a very minor and seemingly insignificant change in the arrangement of glands which made them?

Now, to those who would simply reduce the phenomena to a

principle of nature, Paley responds that the term *principle* is merely a name describing a diversified and progressive operation. "The power in organized bodies, of producing bodies like themselves, is one of these principles. Give a philosopher this and he can get on." But he adds that the same philosopher does not reflect what such a mode of production (or such a *principle*) requires for the ultimate result to occur. And because this whole miraculous system of reproduction can be grouped under one single term or concept called *generation*, it is simply written off as a fundamental principle of nature. "The truth is, generation is not a principle, but a *process*." He writes that if we can call reproduction a principle we might as well call the casting of metals, or spinning and weaving, principles.

To further destroy the atheistic write off of causal sequences as simply natural *principles*, Paley offers this little classic of a paragraph:

"And, after all, or in what sense is it true, that animals produce their like? A butterfly, with a proboscis instead of a mouth, with four wings and six legs, produces a hairy caterpillar, with jaws and teeth, and fourteen feet. A frog produces a tadpole. A black beetle, with gauze wings, and a crusty covering, produces a white, smooth, soft worm; an ephemeron fly, a cod-bait maggot. These, by a progress through different stages of life, and action, and enjoyment (and, in each state, provided with implements and organs appropriated to the temporary nature which they bear) arrive at last at the form and fashion of the parent animal. But all this is process."

II

There are numerous arguments for the existence of God but there are, to this time, only four philosophical arguments which have withstood rather well under utmost scrutiny. These are known as the Four Great Arguments for the Existence of God. They are the ontological argument, the cosmological (or causal) argument, the teleological argument and the moral argument. They have been with us for thousands of years but in their classic form they were developed by St. Anselm (ontological), St. Thomas Aquinas (cosmological), William Paley (teleological) and Immanuel Kant (moral). Aspects of these *proofs* were touched upon in the preceding section, as, for instance, in discussing cause and effect the subject was cosmology, and in touching upon design in nature the subject was teleology.

Ontology is a division of metaphysics which is concerned with the essence of *being*. It seeks to establish truth by finding fundamental principles which are noncontradictory and to deduce from these principles truth about God and the world (meaning *of all that exists*). In the "theater" of ontology, experience has little place, though, of course, some would argue that it has *no* place at all. What is defined as the *ontological argument* for the existence of God goes along this track: God is something so great that there is nothing that can be conceived to be greater; and something this great, therefore, cannot be conceived of as not existing. If it cannot exist, then it is not so great after all, for it is incapable of possessing that which other things possess: *existence*. This something of which nothing greater can be conceived is God.[3]

Aquinas and others attacked the argument because they reasoned that not everyone who hears the name of God understands it to signify something than which nothing greater can be thought, for there are those of us who see God as merely a physical substance. Besides, Aquinas added, even if one does understand by this name (God) that there is signified something than which nothing greater can be thought, it does not follow that he understands that the name signifies something which actually exists — he may very well accept that it only exists mentally.[4]

Now, cosmology differs from ontology, although it is also a branch of metaphyics. Whereas ontology seeks truth through non-contradictory first principles, cosmology seeks truth by way of speculations about the essential nature of the physical world. The *cosmological* — or *causal* — *arguments* base their proof on the necessity of a first and all-efficient cause. Generally they state that there must have been a first cause of all that is in motion for there is nothing in the physical world that we know of which can actually originate motion and without a first efficient cause there cannot be a series of intermediate causes *or* an ultimate cause.

Kant and others thought the argument worthy of respect but countered that the idea of a first cause cannot be inferred just because one assumes there is no possibility of an infinite series of causes in the universe.[5]

Quite unlike ontology and cosmology is teleology. Teleology is the study of evidence of design in nature. The *teleological argument* for the existence of God, therefore, seeks to prove His existence through a study of nature. It looks not only for evidence of design but for the essential purpose of that design. Wherever there can be found proof of contrivance it follows that there must have been a contriver. Thus, the working parts of each and every existing thing, according to the teleological argument, is ample proof of intelligent and purposeful design. Where there is intelligent design, there must be an inteligent designer.

The major objections to the teleological argument center about the fact that the argument does not prove that there is a creator of the world — at best it simply proves that there is an architect of the world.

The fourth of the great arguments is the *moral argument*. It takes a completely different perspective than the other three. The moral argument is actually a series of arguments which generally infer that there are moral rules which are readily and regularly recognized. These moral rules are so fundamental and so essential in the nature of man that they are, in fact ,moral commands.

The major criticisms of this argument center about the idea of such a moral law. Many philosophers have challenged the entire idea because it infringes on the freedom of man. There is also severe criticism of the argument's inability to establish that even if there were a moral law there must be a moral commander whom we call God.

III

Now, in addition to these four great arguments for God, there are a number of very popular secondary arguments. Among these are the arguments from *common consent, degrees of perfection* and *religious experience.*

The arguments from common consent are based on the almost universal agreement of mankind that there is indeed a supreme being who created and guides the universe. There are few theologians and philosophers who accept this argument as a completely independent and sufficient proof but they accept that when it is combined with all the other arguments it gains even greater weight.

The main objection to this argument is, of course, that belief in God is not truly universal. Buddhists, for one, are the easiest example at which to point. They have no God at all. And in every society, every community, there is often a number of men and women who see no sufficient basis for accepting the idea of a supreme being who actually exists.

The arguments from degrees of perfection are generally similar to those which Aquinas presented in his fourth proof for the existence of

God (*Summa*, Part 1, Question 2, Article 3). Aquinas pointed out that among beings there are degrees of goodness, trueness, nobility, etc. Beings have more or less of these and other qualities. but comparative terms like more or less describe things in relation to some maximum which they are capable of attaining. For example, something is described as hotter if it is closer to being that which is hottest; this same applies to that which is the most noble or the most good. Now when there are circumstances in which many things have a common property, the thing which represents the property in its maximum is the cause of the property in all the other things — as fire, which is the maximum of heat, is the cause of all that is hot. "There must be, therefore, something to which all beings is the cause of their being, goodness, and every other perfection; and this something we call God."[6]

The arguments from degrees of perfection remain fairly well-ignored today except for dedicated Thomists. The general criticism is that the argument only has validity to someone who has already accepted the fact of God's existence.

The last argument with which we will deal is that from *religious experience.* It is based on the feelings and emotions which bring men and women to a realization that indeed God exists. It is not a very concrete argument because it is so subjective. But many writers are quick to point out that the argument carries the weight of numbers. That is, throughout history there have been so many who claimed to come to know, or know of, God through a series of experiences, dreams, or meditations, that the argument carries a force similar to that of common consent.

The main objections to this last type of argument are that it does not present a rational basis for investigation, it accepts the fact of His existence before it begins to seek the proof, and the argument is based on an infinite number of personal experiences that may be the result of anything but divine experience.

IV

Weighing all the arguments given above, one finds strong, but not conclusive, proof of the possibility of God.

But why can we not find definite proof? Why must God be so elusive?

Christian and Jewish theologians would be quick to point to God's transcendental nature. He remains far above man's comprehension. In fact, if man is to be sincere in his approach to the whole idea of God, man must find a way to approach the subject in categories of thought far beyond what he uses in his usual intellectual efforts.

This is to say that the problem in finding God is not that God seeks not to be found but that man has not yet the intellectual or spiritual skills to find Him. He can know of Him, and possibly some things about Him, but man cannot know God in His entirety. He may, as the Christians would believe, be known as Christ, but Christ is not the all of God. Christ was a form of God; he was God as man; he was God as He revealed Himself to man; but God is not simply some physical human form — so even through Christ, God cannot be completely known.

These are, of course, mere speculations. No one can talk with certainty of God, with certainty of His relationship with men and women, and with what men and women can or cannot know of Him.

But if God lies beyond the reach of man (though he may be a part of man or man a part of Him) there are certain attributes which most theologians and many philosophers find it necessary to associate with Him. Among these attributes is unlimitlessness.

Now, to say that God is unlimited is to say that there can be no restrictions on Him except, possibly, in the case of contradictions. This is to say that if he is good, His goodness is unlimited and He cannot be sometimes bad and sometimes good. If God is unlimited, then he must be eternal for limitlessness cannot be dimensional.

In *Physics*,[7] Aristotle discusses motion and explains that it is possible to arrive at the idea of an unmoved mover by considering principles of movement. He writes that all existing things are sometimes in motion, sometimes at rest. Now everything that is in motion is moved by something and the mover is either not moved at all or in motion. if it is in motion it is being moved either by itself or by something else. This is true throughout the series. Thus, we deduct that the first principle causing things to be in motion must be that which moves itself, that first principle, therefore, being *unmoved*.

Through observations, Aristotle continues, we realize there are things which move themselves. These are the members of the animal kingdom and every other living thing. But they move themselves with a motion that is not actually originating from the animal itself. The animal moves itself in connection with other natural motions which they have not originated, such as the internal workings of their body. These internal motions occur whether the animal is at rest or in motion, so the animal, in a true sense, does not operate itself by means of its own agency. "Hence we may confidently conclude that if a thing belongs to the class of unmoved movents that are themselves moved accidently, it is not possible that it should cause continuous motion. So the necessity that there should be motion continuously requires that there should be a first movement that is unmoved even accidently."[8]

Aristotle goes on to imply that if there is indeed a mover that is unmoved, this mover must be eternal.

In his *Metaphysics,*[9] Aristotle treats the subject again from a different perspective. He writes that the first mover of which he speaks must exist out of necessity, and because it exists out of necessity it must be *good.* Here, then, is another necessary attribute of God: *goodness.*

On this principle of goodness in God, Aristotle writes,[10] depends the existence and well-being of the heavens and the world of nature. And from this principle comes a life "such as the best which we enjoy, and enjoy for but a short time (as it is ever in this state, which we cannot be), since its actuality is also pleasure . . . and thinking in itself deals with that which is best in itself, and that which is thinking in the fullest sense with that which is best in the fullest sense. And thought thinks on itself because it shares the nature of the object of thought; for it becomes an object of thought in coming into contact with and thinking its objects, so that thought and object of thought are the same. For that which is capable of receiving the object of thought, i.e. the essence, is thought. But it is active when it possesses this object. Therefore the possession rather than the receptivity is the divine element which thought seems to contain, and the act of contemplation is what is most pleasant and best. If, then, God is always in that good state, in which we sometimes are, this compels our wonder; and if in a better state, this compels it yet more. And God *is* in a better state. *And life also belongs to God; for the actuality of thought is life, and God is that actuality; and God's self-dependent actuality is life most good and eternal. We say therefore that God is a living being, ETERNAL, most good, so that life and duration continuous and eternal belong to God; for this is God."*

In his *Third Ennead,* Plotinus considers God's eternalness in tractate 7, chapter 5. He discusses an Ever-Being that has no capacity to increment or change, for if it did have, it would not be ever-existent.

But perpetuity in itself, he explains, is not enough to qualify someone or something as being eternal. It must also be incapable of any future change, so that at any period in which it is observed it is as it always has been and always will be.

"Imagine, then," he asks, "the state of a being which cannot come away from the vision of this but is forever caught up in it, held by the spell of its grandeur, kept to it by virtue of a nature itself unfailing — or even the state of one that must labour towards eternity by directed effort, but then to rest in it, immoveable at any point, assimilated to it, co-eternal with it, contemplating eternity and the eternal by what is eternal within the self.

"Accepting this as a true account of an eternal, a perdurable Existent — one which never turns to any kind outside itself, that possesses life completely, that has never reached any accession, that is now receiving none and will never receive any — we have, with the statement of perduring Being, the statement also of perdurance and eternity: perdurance being the corresponding state arising from the substratum and inherent in it; eternity is that substratum carrying that state in manifestation.

"Eternity, then, is of the order of the supremely great; it proves on investigation to be identical with God: it may fitly be described as God made manifest, as God declaring what He is, as existence without jolt or change, and therefore as also the firmly living."

In his *Summa Theologica*,[11] Aquinas also answers the question of whether God is eternal. He writes that the idea of eternity follows logically from the concept of immutability just as the idea of time follows logically from the concept of movement. As God is argued to be absolutely immutable, it follows, then, that God is eternal. Eternity, Aquinas adds, is none other than God himself.

In his *Critique of Pure Reason*,[12] Kant discusses the idea of a primal being, which he explains cannot be made up of other beings having an existence which is derivative in any way, for this last supposes the first and thus cannot be constitutive parts of it. It follows, then, he adds that the primal being must be cogitated as simple. The fact that other beings may develop from this primal being is in no way indicative of either a limitation or a division of its true reality. Whatever the highest reality is, it must be considered as the basic source rather than a containment of all that exists; and the manifold nature of all things must be based upon the complete series of events which come from it. "And thus all our sensory powers, and all reality, may be regarded as belonging to this series of effects, while they could not have formed parts of the idea, considered as an aggregate. Pursuing this train of thought, and hypothesizing this idea, we find ourselves authorized to determine of the Supreme Being by way of the simple conception of a highest reality, as *one, simple, all-efficient* eternal, and so on — in one word, to determine it in its unconditional completeness by the aid of all possible predicates. The conception of such a being is the conception of God in the transcendental sense..."

And this God, Aquinas would add,[13] is the only thing which can truly possess eternity. Nothing else which exists can exist from eternity but God! In fact, according to Aquinas, anything which does exist does so only by the will of God. If the universe is to be eternal then it can only be so because God so wills it. Anything, including the very world itself, is necessary only to the extent that it is necessary for God to will it. There is no necessity, that we can imagine, for the world to exist. There is just no possible way for us to demonstrate such necessity. The things of the world exist in the world of time, anyway, and these things are corruptible, they can diminish to extinction, break apart, corrupt entirely, etc. If there is nothing which can exist from eternity but God, that leaves man to exist only in the realm of time. Things which exist in time have a beginning and an end. So, too, then, must man — unless there is someplace between eternity and time especially reserved for him.

IV.

In summary:

The concept of eternity is so bound up with the concept of God that the two subjects are almost indistinguishable. If there is no such thing as eternity then there cannot be this being we call God. If God is not eternal, then He is not, an Anselm insists He must be, "something than which nothing greater can be conceived." If at one time He did not exist well, then, he may at anytime not exist again. But it is absurd to even toy with the idea of a God Who does not possess the attribute of eternalness.

But does He exist? We may accept that if He exists He must be eternal, but we need not accept that he does truly exist. Are there any philosophical proofs of His existence?

There are what is called the *four great arguments* for the existence of God. These are the ontological, cosmological, teleological and moral arguments.

The ontological argument stresses the point thusfar made: God is something so great that we cannot possibly think of anyting being greater; and something this great, therefore, cannot be conceived as not existing, for if it cannot exist it is less than you or I, for we at least possess existence. If it is less than you or I, it cannot be God.

The cosmological argument states that there must have been a first cause of all motion for there is nothing we know of which can actually originate motion, and without a first cause there cannot be a series of intermediate causes or a final cause. The first cause is that which we call God.

The teleological argument for the existence of God seeks to prove His existence by evidences of design in nature. Wherever we an find proof of design it follows that there must have been a designer. This designer is that which we define as God.

The moral argument is actually a series of arguments which infer that there are moral rules or "commands" which are generally recognized by mankind. If there does indeed exist "moral commands" then it stands to reason that there must be a moral commander. This moral commander is that which we refer to as God.

Each of these arguments have met with its share of criticism, some of which follow: the ontological because if it is valid we can expect the existence of any idea which comes to mind as the greatest of its kind; the cosmological because we cannot infer that there is indeed a first cause just because we believe there is no possibility of an infinite ascending series of causes and effects; the moral argument because the idea of general moral "commands" is highly arguable. But the fact that these arguments have met with criticism does not necessarily render them invalid. One must also weigh the logical force of the criticism against the weight of the arguments. The debate on the value of the arguments goes on from generation to generation with one proof losing or gaining ground over the others as scholars reach new insights.

But in addition to these four great arguments there are others which are based on the almost universal agreement of mankind that God exists, on the personal and religious experience of men and women, and on other rational arguments such as Aquinas' *degrees of perfection.*

In any event, the evidences, though not conclusive, are overwhelmingly in favor of the existence of God. Whether or not one single argument will ever be proof enough, or whether or not there will ever be any argument sufficient to satisfy all intellects, is anyone's guess.

But though we can know of Him, perhaps, by metaphysical investigation or religious experience, there is little we can know about Him for his transcendent nature brings him far beyond our ability to comprehend.

However, we can rationalize that He must possess certain attributes, among them, *goodness* and *eternalness*.

As Aristotle writes in his *Metaphysics:* " ... life belongs to God; for the actuality of thought is life, and God is that actuality; and God's self-dependent actuality is life most good and eternal. We say, therefore, that God is a living being, eternal, most good ..... "

CHAPTER 3
Between Time and Eternity

That the particular being whom we have come to name God should possess eternalness is necessary to our concept of Him. As Paley indicates in Chapter 24 of *Natural Theology,* we perceive God as being omnipotent, omniscient, omnipresent, eternal and self-existing.

If we subscribe to the notion that He is not only the prime mover of all that exists in the universe but also the *creator* of the universe, we cannot deny his omnipotence. After all, some single being capable of creating the heavens and the earth in all their vast complexity and able to design and create all inanimate and animate forms in the world (as well as to contrive relationships amongst these forms so as to make the world self-sufficient) must have powers that are beyond any we can imagine or hope to understand once we have identified them.

In regard to his omniscience, any investigation into the intricacies of our world and its inhabitants is proof enough of His incredible knowledge. In regard to his omnipresence, we have this proof offered by Paley:[1] "In every part and place of the universe with which we are acquainted, we perceive the exertion of a power, which we believe, mediately or immediately, to proceed from the Deity. For instance, in what part of point of space that has ever been explored do we not discover attraction . . . What kingdom is there of nature, what corner of space, in which there is anything that can be examined by us, where we do not fall upon contrivance and design."

Of course, omnipotence and omniscience in no way guarantee eternalness. God could very well have been an accident of time and place. But Paley assures us that He is no accident, for if He did indeed contrive the universe and the things which exist in it, he must be eternal. This is because, when one gets right down to it, eternity is a negative idea in that it "is the negation of a beginning or an end." Echoing Aquinas, Paley explains that there never could have been a time when nothing existed because, if so, such a time must continue. "The universal *blank* must have remained, nothing could rise up out of it; nothing could exist now. In strictness, however, we have no concern prior to that of the visible world. Upon this article therefore of theology, it is sufficient to know, that the contriver necessarily existed before the contrivance."[2]

Now, just as eternity is a negative idea, so, too, is self-existence, Paley adds, for it implies there was no preceding cause, no other maker, no author of He whom we refer to as God. There was at one instant in the course of eternity only God. This is, of course, no easy concept to grasp!

It is quite easy to accept that if there is indeed a supreme being, he is eternal in nature and, being self-existent, depending on no other for either his formation or his continuance, there is nothing which can terminate his existence. But because this supreme being came from eternity, *is* eternity, He therefore is indestructible. But what about you and I and every man and woman walking, working, playing on earth. We are not a part of eternity; we have been born into another state, a state of temporal things, a state where things born to it are eventually corrupted into non-existence, a state called *time*. What does the future hold for us? Born into time, must we one day cease to be? All our work and effort, growth and knowledge obtained for no future personal benefit?

Is there any possibility that there may exist a third state, a state in which things not existing eternally may be born into eternity? It is, after all, clearly evident that only God is eternal and has the privilege of *ever-afterness*.

II

In addition to the concepts of eternity and time, there is also the concept of another state or dimension which exists between the two. It is called aeviternity. It may be distinguished from eternity and time by this comparison: eternity has neither a beginning nor an end, time has both a beginning and an end, *aeviternity has a beginning and no end*. Aquinas adds in his *Summa Theologica*[3] that they are distinguished one from the other because: eternity has *no before* and *no after,* time has a *before* and *after* plus *newness* and *oldness,* aeviternity has a *before* and *after* but no *newness* and *oldness.*

Aquinas goes on to explain that "We say . . . that since eternity is the measure of a permanent being, in so far as anything recedes from permanence of being it recedes from eternity. Now some things recede from permanence of being, so that their being is subject to change, or consists in change; and these things are measured by time, as are all movements, and also the being of all things corruptible.

But others recede less from permanence of being, because their being neither consists in change, nor is the subject of change; nevertheless they have change annexed to them either actually, or potentially.

"This appears in the heavenly bodies, the substantial being of which is unchangeable; and yet along with unchangeable being they have changeableness of place. The same applies to the angels who have an unchangeable being with changeableness as regards choice, which pertains to their nature; moreover they have changeableness of intelligence, of affections, and of places in their own degree. Therefore these are measured by aeviternity, which is a mean between eternity and time. But the being that eternity measures is not changeable, nor is it joined to change. In this way time has before and after; aeviternity in itself has no before and after, but they can be joined to it; while eternity has neither before nor after, nor is it at all compatible with such."

Augustine acknowledges a state in-between eternity and time but not so directly as Aquinas. In his *Confessions*[4] he speaks of things which, though they are not coeternal with God will share in his eternity and are given ability to rise above the changeableness of time. He writes (his format being an address to God):[5]

" . . . two things I find that Thou has made, not within the compass of time, neither of which is coeternal with Three. One which is so formed that, without any ceasing of contemplation, without any interval of change, though changeable, yet not changed, it may thoroughly enjoy thy eternity and unchangeableness; the other which was so formless that it had not that which could be changed from one form into another, whether of motion or of repose, so as to become subject unto time. But this thou didst not leave thus formless, because before all days Thou in the beginning didst create Heaven and Earth; the two things that I spake of. But the Earth was invisible and without form, and darkness was upon the deep. In which words is the formless conveyed unto us (that such capacities may hereby be drawn on by degrees, as are not able to conceive an utter privation of all form, without yet coming to nothing) out of which another Heaven might be created together with a visible and well-formed earth: and the waters diversely ordered, and whatsoever further is in the formation of the world recorded to have been, not without days, created; and that, as being of such nature, the successive changes of times may take place in them, as being subject to appointed alterations of motions and of forms."

So, if the souls of men and women are indeed immortal as Socrates would claim, then they cannot exist from eternity for, as Aquinas writes, nothing other than God can be from eternity; and souls cannot exist in time for time not only has a before but also an after. They must exist in another dimension or state, which Augustine and Aquinas have defined for us as being *aeviternity.*

III

The question which immediately comes to perplex individuals contemplating immortality is how we are actually able to transcend death. After all, it is clear that when one dies every part of the body eventually decays. What is the soul without a body? Is it possible for God to raise the dead?

Paley offers some interesting ideas on just how God might be able to give life continued and individual existence even after death.[6]

Any plant or animal begins from an incredibly minute particle. Yet as small as this particle may be — so small as not even to be visible by the naked eye — it contains within it the complete organization of a future body. This incredibly tiny, and for all practical purposes *invisible,* particle determines whether that which is about to come into being will be a rational creature as you or I, a humble animal such as a frog, or a gigantic tulip tree. And this minute particle has itself been born of a prior body. Yet "the incepted organization, though formed within, and through, and by, a preceding organization, is not corrupted by its corruption, or destroyed by its dissolution; but, on the contrary, is sometimes extricated and developed by those very causes; survives and comes into action, when the purpose, for which it was prepared, requires its use." Paley continues that this special economy that nature has developed for the transference of an organization from one individual to another, "may have something analogous to it, when the purpose is to transmit an organization from one state of being to another state." To those who feel that this transference cannot be of a *true* individual because the mind depends on organization and death is the corrupter of that organization, Paley points out that "whatever can transmit a similarity of organization will answer their purpose, because, according even to their own theory, it may be the vehicle of consciousness . . . because consciousness carries identity and individuality along with it through all changes of form or visible qualities." The main point Paley is making is that a God who can design a tiny particle to develop into something which in no way resembles anything visibly discernible in that particle clearly has the power to "mould and fashion the parts of material nature, so as to fulfil any purpose whatever . . . " And that includes the raising of the individual from the dead, the transporting of him from a temporal to an immortal state.

Paley never held that the soul was indeed a physical thing but he sought to give a natural argument to those who failed to see the power of God. Paley saw God as being spiritual. Spirituality, he explained, was both a negative and a positive idea — negative in the sense that it excluded some material properties and positive because it implied thought and power: the origination of motion. Spirit was superior to matter as the last cannot move unless it be moved. The soul as the connection between man and God would also be of a spiritual nature and its transference from one state of existence to another need not have any natural explanation.

IV

Regarding the body as purely a mechanism for use by the soul, William Paley wrote in Chapter 9 of *Natural Theology:* "I have sometimes wondered why we are not struck with mechanism in animal bodies as readily and as strongly as we are struck with it, at first sight, in a watch or a mill."

But he was not simply raising an open-ended question. This was never Paley's style. He had a possible answer to the dilemma. The reason just might be, he says, that animal bodies are for the most part made up of unusually soft and elastic substances — flabbly substances, he calls them — like muscles, membranes, skin, veins, arteries, etc. And we are quite accustomed to mechanical items configured from hard materials like wood or metal. "There is something therefore of habit in the case," he concludes, "but it is sufficiently evident that there can be no proper reason for any distinction of the sort. Mechanism may be displayed in the one kind of substance as well as in the other."

A perspective such as this is one that sets holy men, present and past, and true lovers of mankind apart from all others. They have always envisioned a body as a vehicle for use by the soul. Their love of others on a very individual basis has never been limited to simply physical attractions or social concerns. They have looked beyond the physical configuration of individuals, into their minds or souls, and it is at this depth that they have always dealt with individuals. This is also why we can believe that priests and brothers of the Church, of all those who are celibate by vow in any religion can fully adhere to the restrictions which are imposed on them by their own choosing. This is not to say that we do not hear of, or find on occasion, that certain individuals under the vow of chastity, have disregarded that vow at certain times, but this is generally because the free expression of their desires have been carried too well into their new lives through force of habit and they cannot pull the reins on these habits too quickly or too completely, or else, in moments of human weakness or overpowering curiosity, they find themselves questioning the validity of their vows.

V

In summary:

Some philosophers and theologians accept the existence of a state that exists "between" time and eternity. This they call aeviternity. Things which are born into this state of existence have, of course, had a beginning, but they will have no end.

God exists in *eternity* for he has had *no beginning* and will have *no end.* The world exists in *time* for it has had a *beginning* and will surely have an *end.* But man, or at least the soul of man, exists in *aeviternity,* for while man has had a *beginning,* he will have *no end.*

CHAPTER 4
The Soul in Time and Eternity

In Greek mythology there existed, about the 7th Century B.C., an itinerant poet and philosopher whose music and teaching treated the creation of the universe and the afterlife which belonged to the soul. His name or Orpheus. Those who accepted his teachings as truth believed that the soul of every man and women would be held responsible for his or her life on earth, would receive reward or punishment according to the merits of that life, and would eventually be reincarnated into another body.

Whether or not Orpheus ever existed is quite beside the point. The writings and stories attributed to him had an important impact on a noted philosopher who was born about 570 B.C. His name was Pythogoras. He developed further the idea that the psyche — or soul — of man was not mortal at all but rather a part of some universal force from which it had become separated and eventually imprisoned within some mortal form. The Pythogorean way of life became, then, one which was preoccupied with the soul rather than the body, one which was dedicated to training the soul for the day when it would return to its eternal parent.

Pythogorean ideas on both philosophy and religion, in its turn, had a tremendous influence on Plato, who adopted, among others, Pythogorean arguments for the immortality of the soul. One may, of course, point to Plato's *Symposium* and debate his willingness to accept the soul's immortality; but one may also point to his *Meno* where he argues, through Socrates, for the eternal nature of the soul.

There is a scene in *Meno* where Socrates and Meno are involved in a series of dialogues that eventually leads Meno to ask Socrates exactly what he (Socrates) means when he says that what we call learning is actually only *recollection.* You see, Socrates believed that the soul is eternal and that it has been born into mortal form many times; it has, therefore, seen and learned all things. One cannot teach it anyting new, then, but only help it to remember.

Meno doubts this so Socrates decides to illustrate his point. He asks Meno to call one of his attendants to him. Meno does so and Socrates proceeds to question the boy on some points in geometry.

Socrates draws a square (see figure 1) and asks the boy if he understands the definition of a square and that all its sides must be

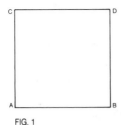

FIG. 1

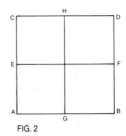

FIG. 2

equal. He then draws a couple of lines through the square (as in figure 2) and points out that these lines must also be equal. The boy agrees to all of this.

In answering Socrates' next series of questions, the boy acknowledges:

1. that the figure could indeed be larger or smaller and still remain a square.

2. that if one side is two feet long and the other side, also, the whole square becomes twice two feet. That is to say that it is then four feet in area.

But then Socrates asks him: "If the first figure has a side of two feet and the second figure is double that, what is the size of the second figure?

"Double that," the boy answers. "Obviously, Socrates, it will be double that in size."

Socrates then turns to Meno and asks him if he understands that Socrates is not actually teaching the boy anything, only asking him questions. Meno replies that he understands this.

"Now," Socrates comments, "he believes he knows the size of the eight-foot square. But does he know?"

"Of course not," Meno replies.

And the boy truly does not know, for he firmly believes it to be twice the length of the first. Thus, Socrates has demonstrated to this point that the boy has some definite misconceptions. He *does not* know the size of the second figure.

Now, Socrates will order his questions so that, without receiving the true answer from Socrates, the boy will come to understand that he does indeed *not* know. Remember, now, at this point the boy firmly believes he knows the answer.

But before he constructs the questions that will lead the boy to acknowledge his ignorance he questions him in a manner that reviews exactly what the boy believes. The boy believes that the side which is of double length from that in the first figure will produce a figure which is double the size of the first. This is providing, of course, that the second figure is equal on all sides like the first, except that it is double in size and, therefore, as the first is four feet this second must be eight feet.

If this is true, Socrates says, by extending *AB* a length equal to its present size one has a line double the length of *AB*, does he not? (See figure 3).

An easy enough question. The boys answers yes. And he further agrees that:

1. if line *AB* is extended a length equal to its size, AB is now double its size.
2. the eight foot square would be made by making three more lines of the same length.

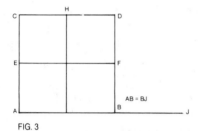

FIG. 3

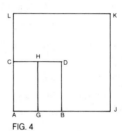

FIG. 4

Socrates draws in three equal lines (Figure 4) using the first line as the base for the new figure. And he asks the boy if this did not, therefore, give them what the boy would call an eight-foot figure.

The boy answers yes. Socrates then asks if it does not contain four additional squares (Figure 5), each equal to the original four foot one. The boy answers yes and Socrates, in turn, replies that shouldn't it then be four times as big? The boy replies in the affirmative.

"And is four times the same as twice?" asks Socrates.

"No, it is not," replies the boy.

"So the doubling of the side has not given us a double figure but a fourfold figure?"

The boy admits this is true.

"And four times four are sixteen, are they not?" Socrates asks.

"Yes."

"Then," Socrates asks, "how big is the side of the eight-foot square? This one has given us four times the original area, has it not?"

Again the boy answers in the affirmative and he agrees that a side half the length has given them a square of four feet.

"And is not a square of eight feet double that of four feet and half that of sixteen?"

"Yes."

"Well, now, does the eight foot square not have a side greater than that of the four feet square and less than that of the sixteen feet square?"

"Yes."

"Then the side of the eight-feet square must be longer than two feet but shorter than four?"

"It must be."

"And how long must it be, then?"

"Three feet."

Socrates then asks the boy that if this is so, can they take half of line *BJ* and define it as being three feet in length. The boy says yes. Socrates then follows the same pattern he used before to construct a second square; he draws four more within it (Figure 5). Then he turns to Meno and says: "Notice now how, though in a state of complete perplexity, he will discover the truth by seeking it with my help, though I simply question him without teaching him."

Next, Socrates asks how many times larger AEJG (See Figure 6) is this ABCD. The boy answers four. Socrates then asks him if it is not their objective to come up with a square *not four times* the size of the first but only double. Now he cuts the squares in half with connecting diagonal lines (Figure 7).

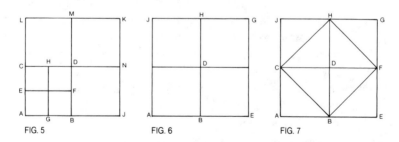

FIG. 5   FIG. 6   FIG. 7

"Are the lines (BFHC), which enclose the area, equal?" he asks. The boy replies that they are. Then Socrates asks him to consider just how big this area must be. "There are four squares," he says. "Have not the lines (BFHC) cut off the inner half of each of them?"

"Yes." And in answer to Socrates' next question, the boy acknowledges that there are four halves in the new figure and two in ABCD; as the relationship of four to two is double, this figure must be eight feet."

"On what base?" asks Socrates and the boy answers that base is on the line which goes from one corner to another on the square of four feet.

"So, then, you are of the opinion that the square on the diagonal of the original square is double its area?" Socrates asks.

"Yes, that is so."

Socrates turns to Meno and asks him if the boy has answered any of Socrates' questions with opinions that weren't his own. Meno admits that all opinions expressed belonged solely to the boy.

"But he did not know the correct answer a few minues ago, as you had agreed," Socrates says to Meno. "So, therefore, a man who does not know does have within himself true opinions on a subject, although he does not have knowledge of it."

Meno agrees and Socrates continues: "At present, these opinions, having been newly aroused, possess a dreamlike quality. But if these same questions are given to him on many occasions and in different ways, you can see that he will finally have a knowledge of the subject which is accurate as any other."

Meno admits that this is probably true.

"But this knowledge," explains Socrates, "will come not from teaching but from interrogation. The boy will recover what knowledge is existent completely by himself. And this spontaneous recovery of knowledge that is already within him is recollection, is it not?"

"Yes," Meno answers.

"Then, he has either achieved the knowledge of which he is now in possession, or else he has always been in possession of it. If it it true that he has always possessed it, then he must have always been knowing it; but if, on the other hand, he came into acquiring it at some other previous time, it cannot ossibly have been during this lifetime, unless he has been taught geometry. He will always respond in the same way with geometric knowledge as well as with any subject. But has there been anyone who has taught all of this to him?"

Meno replies that no person has ever taught these things to the boy, yet he does possess these true opinions. To this Socrates replies that if the boy did not acquire his knowledge, it must be immediately clear that he had possessed and/or learned it during some other period of existence."

"This would seem to be so," Meno agrees.

"And this would have to be when he was not in human form?"

"Yes."

"If, then," Socrates continued, "there are going to exist within him, both when he is and when he is not a man, those true opinions that can be aroused by questioning and converting into knowledge, can we not say that *his soul has been forever in a state of knowledge?* For truly, he has always been either a man or not a man."

"True."

"And if the truth about the reality of things is always contained in our soul, the soul must be immortal . . ."

Here Socrates has argued more for the eternity of the soul than simply its immortality. But what he as effectively pointed out, is that there is a possibility that our souls — or whatever we wish to call that essential part of ourselves which cannot be divided or destroyed — has existed in some prior time.

Plato's argument for immortality of the soul is also really an argument for the eternalness of the soul. In *Phaedrus* he explains that the soul in all her being is immortal, for it is forever in motion, and that which is forever in motion is immortal. "Only the self-moving, never leaving self, never ceases to move," he writes, "and is the beginning of motion to all that moves besides. Now, the beginning cannot be begotten, for that which is begotten needs to have had a beginning; but the beginning is begotten of nothing, for it is begotten of something then the begotten would not come from a beginning. But if something is unbegotten then it must also be indestructible; for if beginning were to be destroyed, then there could be no beginning out of anything, nor anything out of a beginning; and everything must have a beginning. And, therefore, that which is self-moving, is the beginning of motion."[1]

The self-moving, Plato claims, can neither be terminated nor begotten — otherwise the universe would collapse and be motionless, never again to exist. "But if the self-moving is proven immortal," he adds, "he who confirms that self-motion is necessary to the essence of the soul will have no confusion. For that body which is moved from without has no soul; but that body which is moved from within is with soul, for this is the nature of the soul. And if this be true, *is not the soul self-moving, and necessarily unbegotten and immortal?*"[2]

II

In the Fourth Ennead, Seventh Tractate, Plotinus also discusses the immortality of the soul. He writes that man is made up of both a soul and a body. The body, however, is not everlasting for there are many things which can pervert, wreck and totally destroy it. Bodies are simply material forms and like all material forms they are temporary. If the body is really a part of the essence of man, then man cannot be immortal. However, if the body is simply a material supply to that which we generally refer to as man, an instrument for use in this world — ah, well, then the body is not really a part of man and its passing is not the passing of the man. He can continue on without it. That which we call the soul must have life ingrained in it; but it must consist of two or more bodies; that life, then, will be vested, either in all those bodies or in one of them to the exclusion of the other or others; if this is not so, then there is no life present anywhere."

According to Plotinus, if any of these bodies contain this ingrained life, that body is the one which is the soul. He also states that body itself cannot possibly exist in any form whatever if that thing we might call soul-power did not exist, for bodies pass on — dissolution is a necessary part of their nature — and all would eventually be obliviated in no time at all if everything were simply body. Because all bodies are in a ceaseless recession into dissolution, if the cosmos were made over to them it would float in meaningless drift, having no order, no reason, no intelligence. "But given soul, all material things become collaborators with the life principle to bring about an orderly cosmos; but without soul in the things of the universe, these things could not even exist let alone perform their functions."[3]

According to Plotinus, then, bodies cannot exist without soul; but souls can exist without body.

III

In his *Summa Theologica*,[4] Aquinas also considers the question of whether the soul consists of both matter and form. He explains that the question may be considered from two perspectives. The first is from the general idea of a soul which sees it as simply a form of a body. "Now," he writes, "it is either a form of virtue of itself in its entirety or by virtue of some part of itself. If it is a form of virtue in its entirety, then it is not possible that any part of it can be matter, if by matter we understand some being only in potency, for a form, as such, is an act; and that which is only in potency cannot be part of an act, since potency is contrary to act as being its opposite. If, however, it be a form of virtue of a part of itself, then that part of it we call the soul —and that matter, which it actualizes first, we call the first thing animated.

"Secondly, we may proceed from the notion of the human soul in particular, in so far as it has intellect. Now, it is clear that whatever is received into something is received according to the condition of the recipient and a thing is known as far as its form is in the knower. But the intellectual soul knows a thing in its nature absolutely; for instance, it knows a stone absolutely as a stone; and therefore the form of a stone absolutely, as to its own formed notion, is in the intellectual soul. Therefore the intellectual soul itself is an absolute form and not something composed of matter and form. For if the intellectual soul were composed of matter and form, the forms of things would be received into it as individuals, and so it would only know the individual; just as it happens with the sensitive powers which receive forms in a corporeal organ, since matter is the principle by which forms are individualized. It follows, therefore, that the intellectual soul, and every intellectual substance which has knowledge of forms absolutely, is without composition of matter and form."

But, Aquinas goes on to explain, the soul cannot operate properly without the body. The soul needs a phantasm in order for it to find meaning in anything, in order for it to have any understanding. And quoting Aristotle, he stresses that "there is no phantasm without the body."

But while the soul requires the body in order for it to be able to understand things, the soul continues to exist without the body. The soul is definitely incorruptible, he insists, and offers the following argument to prove his point.

"For a thing may be corrupted in two ways — in itself and accidently. Now it is impossible for any subsistent being to be generated or corrupted accidently, that is, by the generation or corruption of something else. For generation and corruption belong to a thing in the same way that being belongs to it, which is acquired by generation and lost by corruption. Therefore, whatever has being in itself cannot be generated or corrupted except in itself; while things which do not subsist, such as accidents and material forms, acquire being or lose it through the generation of corruption of composites. Now it was shown above that the souls of brutes are not self-subsistent, whereas the human soul is, so that the souls of brutes are corrupted when their bodies are corrupted, while the human soul could not be corrupted unless it were corrupted in itself." Aquinas continues on to explain that this is not only true of the soul but true of anything subsistent that is a form alone. He points out that what belongs to a thing by virtue of the very nature of that thing has got to be inseparable from it. "But being belongs to a form, which is an act, by virtue of itself. And, thus, matter acquires actual being according as it acquires form; while it is corrupted so far as the form is separated from it. But it is impossible for a form to be separated from itself; and therefore it is impossible for a subsistent form to cease to exist."[5]

IV

In summary:

Even in ancient Greece there were sects which accepted the immortality of the soul. One of these sects was led by the poet-philosopher Orpheus. Whether or not he actually existed, the writing attributed to him had a powerful impact on the ideas of Pyhogoras whose teachings, in turn, came to influence Plato.

Many philosophers from ancient times to medieval times and even to the current generation have observed that man consists of two separate things, one which is body and is corruptible, and the other which is soul and cannot be corrupted. But this is not to say that there are not many men and women of good mind and strong standing in the fields of philosophy who do not argue to the contrary, that whatever man is, or whatever it is he consists of, at bodily death he dies completely.

Aquinas, whose arguments ended the previous sub-chapter, and whose ideas guide 600 million Catholics besides other Christian philosophers, and who is respected in all quarters by men and women in philosophy — though they may challenge some of his ideas — especially saw man as consisting of an incorruptible soul but cor-ruptible body.

He argued that the soul comes into being when the body is born. It needs the body for it is only through this physical form that it can come to understand God and the world. But it needs the body only for understanding and is not dependent upon it for survival. The soul exists in aeviternity, and things which are aeviternal have no end.

CHAPTER 5
Nature and Immortality of the Soul

There is an insurmountable problem for most individuals in whole-heartedly accepting the idea of the soul's immortality. It is the same one that prevents one from unconditionally accepting the existence of God (unless he or she is given to accepting His existence on faith alone). It is this: there is no one who has seen, touched, or heard the voice of God, or, if there is or has been someone, he or she is unable to offer indisputable proof of the experience. Being physical beings (also), the only things of which we can be certain are those which we have experienced. Everything else we accept conditionally based on the facts we have or the credibility of the witnesses or teachers who inform us. If someone tells me you exist I will accept it until there is sufficient proof that you do not. However, if I experience you through any of my senses no amount of conflicting evidence will prove to me that you do not exist.

Just as no one can prove having seen or touched God, no one has seen, touched, or in anyway physically sensed this part of every human being we call the soul. Does it exist?

There are some unique problems in discussing the soul. These have to do with the religious connotation and the varied interpretations of such synonyms as "mind" or "psyche". Mention soul to anyone and they immediately expect the conversation or debate to continue on strictly religious rather than philosophical grounds. The word "soul" in itself then, presents obstacles to serious discussions about personal immortality.

We face a similar dilemma when we speak of that driving force behind the brain's activity that we call the "mind," often used as a synonym for "soul" but also often used interchangeably with the word "brain." Many scientists see the word mind as no more than a term defining the total activity of the brain. Nonetheless, there is something which appears to be more than the sum of the human parts, a something that would even drive the natural instincts to destroy what they are ordinarily designed to preserve, and this we have come to call "mind". But, unfortunately, to many individuals the word "mind" represents a physical, and therefore, corruptible thing and this understanding immediately negates any idea of the mind's immortality.

The word "psyche" also has inherent problems. It comes into play often in psychological writings and individuals tend to associate it with the fundamental motivation of the individual rather than to the fundamental nature of that individual. To many, then, the psyche is as temporary as anything in the temporal order.

There is, then, little choice, actually, but to continue to use the word "soul" to describe that fundamental and immaterial characteristic of every man or woman which is unchanging and immortal and which is essentially whom they are.

Many individuals would argue, "Listen, let's face it. We are highly sophisticated animals but animals nonetheless. We are physical creatures. We are born, grow older and stronger, then older and weaker until we die and our physical remains disintegrate."

Others would argue, "But, wait. There is something within us that drives this physical body and uses it to achieve certain ends. If I were just a sophisticated animal I would only work to my own special satisfactions. But I recognize that there is something within me that transcends simply physical needs and that there is something which transcends the me that you know. For instance, I know that when I am generous regardless of the consequences to myself, helpful to others despite the physical sacrifice I must endure, and willing to go hungry so others might eat, there must be something which transcends my animal and selfish nature. My body is a machine which is excellently designed to run without my constant supervision and which knows how to feed and defend itself. What, then, is there about me that can make this body go against itself? And yet when I make this body react against itself I do not feel that I am working against that thing I call "me." And if there is this force which uses and drives my body, it must transcend it. It can very well live on without it. It can very well be immortal.

II

Now, if the arguments for such a thing as an eternal state are valid, there is indeed an argument for the continued existence of the soul. But this does not necessarily mean that there is an argument for the continuance of the individual. In other words, if there is eternal existence and eternity and God are one, we may very well have the opportunity to share in that eternity but not as the individuals we are today. This is not a very attractive thought and the fact that we have been granted individuality is in itself argument that we will continue to have the privilege of being distinct. But there are those who will teach us that we are simply ideas in the mind of God which have been allowed to exist and in the end of time we will once again become incorporated into His essence.

Thus, our eternalness is no argument for individual continuance. However, the argument for immortality is, for the idea of immortality lends itself to a completely different interpretation. Immortality means not just simply continuing to be but continuing to be as very distinct individuals. This may be the significance of Aquinas' argument for an aeviternal state. That which has been created in aeviternity has the guarantee of immortality. As that soul which is created in aeviternity is distinct from others, one would assume it would remain not only immortal but also distinct.

The idea of the body simply being a machine which is used by another substance in its search for understanding and, perhaps, in its need for communication, is an idea not unlike that which Socrates presented thousands of years ago. He pointed out that there is something which uses the special features of the physical body and because the user of a thing cannot be the thing itself, it must be distinct. Socrates calls the thing which uses the physical body the "soul."

III

Socrates was neither the first nor the last philospher to look upon the body as simply a mechanical device — as soft and flexible as it might be — which is there as a vehicle for the soul. The idea is an intriguing one in philosophy, although today, with the advances in computer technology and scientific research the tendency is turning toward a more atheistic and temporal rather than deistic and eternal view. Technologists look at the computer and tend to recognize man as one; scientists look into the human brain and see in it the possibility that the mind is a part of it rather than it a part of the mind.

But on investigation, or rather *reflection,* there is so much about the human body that appears simply mechanical that it is hard to picture it as being its own driving, or guiding, force. One is tempted to make an analogy between a soul and its body and a driver and his car. Picture in your mind, if you will, a new automobile. Assume further that you are the owner or, at least, the driver of this fantastic machine. You have not constructed the vehicle; in fact, you probably do not even understand its mechanism; but you can learn, or have learned, how to use similar vehicles and you can apply your knowledge quite easily to this one.

When you step into the vehicle, turn on its ignition and drive off, you are simply involved in navigating it. You steer, accelerate, brake, turn. The engine and all the working parts of the car function quite independently of you. This is to say, it makes little difference to the car whether you or someone else is driving it: press this button and the horn blows, turn this wheel and the car goes left, hit this pedal and the car stops. You are not involved in the eternal workings of the car. You need not know what a piston is, or a carburetor, or a spark plug, or a distributor, or a transmission. All these parts perform their function according to the plan laid out by a rather ingenious designer.

Consider simply the engine of the car. You may think you make the car go but it is the engine, which you may never lay your eyes on or understand, which moves the machine. What you actually do is make the decisions for the machine: when to go, when to stop, when and where to turn and how sharply, etc. But the engine moves the car and is itself actually moved by the art of the original designer who no longer must play a part in its operation and may go about at anyone of his million preoccupations, knowing well the car will respond to your commands.

And that engine is a rather sophisticated bit of engineering. In the gasoline engine, the design is such that the burning of the fuel releases thermal energy to be converted into mechanical energy. This engine, of course, requires a device called a carburetor which allows air to mix with the gasoline. This combination of air and gasoline produces a flammable mixture which is eventually ignited by the electrodes from a spark plug. (The spark plug is itself a simple enough device but generally well-beyond the understanding of most drivers who are neither able to comprehend its function or, if they are able to comprehend it, cannot construct one or replace one. But such knowledge is not required of an individual before he qualifies as a driver.) Gas which has come to be formed in the cylinder as a result of the necessary mix of gasoline and air causes the crankshaft to turn by putting downward pressure on a piston connected to that crankshaft by a rod. Used gas must then be forced out and replaced by a new mixture of gas and air. This work is accomplished by a flywheel so designed and situated that it has salvaged some of the mechanical energy released from within the cylinder.

All this and more is happening internally when your automobile is in operation. "All well and good," you will reply to this explanation.

"I'm quite impressed with the way the engine works. It is, indeed, a remarkable contrivance. But you see, all I need to know is where to put the ignition key, where the steering wheel is, and what pedal works what. The way the car has been engineered takes care of all the details so I can get to where I am going with nil amount of engineering knowledge."

And it is a good thing, too, for if it were up to us, with our limited knowledge of the technical sciences, to construct our own automobiles or else have a pedal, switch and button to control all internal functions, we would probably get to our destinations a lot faster if we walked.

Paley, if he were alive today, and other proponents of the teleological argument for the existence of God, would be quick to point out that the body, or any animal form, was nothing more than a very special means of transportation — a lot more complex than a car, of course, but a vehicle of sorts, nonetheless. The problem with coming to realize this, some would argue, is that we are tied so closely to the body, feel every part of it, that it is hard to separate ourselves from it. The thought of us being separate in anyway from our physical form is too great an idea to grasp and certainly an idea which has no sufficient argument to prove it anymore than an idea. We think of ourselves automatically as body-and-soul; to propose that the two are separate, the one being temporal and the other eternal is a nice exercise in metaphysics but something which many feel is beyond proof.

But in terms of beginning a comparison between natural and mechanical contrivances, if one were to simply consider the body's engine, or pump, — that is, the heart — with all its veins and arteries, he or she becomes immediately aware of the sophisticated design that has taken place. Did the heart with all its parts, and these parts interrelating with other organs through veins and arteries, simply come to be by chance?

The heart is made up of a muscle of extraordinary design. Whereas in other parts of the body we find two main types of muscle, the voluntary type of the skeletal system and the involuntary type of other internal organs, in the heart we find a muscle combining the features of involuntary and voluntary muscles. The contraction of the heart muscle begins the necessary rhythm for maintaining the heart and driving the blood through the body. All of this is irrelevant to everyone because they need not know a thing about their heart's internal workings to keep their body going. Some will argue, as

49

William Paley and other teleologians, that the heart alone is sufficient sign of a master designer as here we have a vital organ prepared to function on its own and so intricately constructed that care was even given to the structure of the muscle with which is must operate, a muscle combining the qualities of two different types found in the human system; others will argue that it came to be by an evolution of thousands or millions of years, by a *principle of order* in nature.

One may continue to investigate the design and function of the heart, observing its complex system of veins, the function of its right and left auricles, and those tiny little valves that always open and close at just the right moment, thus assuring that the blood flows in the proper direction to make it to the lungs in time to be mixed with just the right amount of oxygen, and all this occurs in much the same way that, in the car, the gasoline is mixed efficiently with air so the engine can operate.

"All well and good," you might say, just as you did in reply to the explanation of how an automobile engine is designed. "I'm quite impessed with the way the heart works. It is indeed a remarkable contrivance. But you see, all I need to know, is what I want to do next. The way my body has been engineered takes care of all the details so I can get to where I am going with absolutely no knowledge of biology."

The the heart and every part of the body, and the body as a whole, is a magnificent piece of engineering no one will deny. But that this fantastic bit of engineering contains, or is contained by, an element having a separate and immortal nature is too absurd for them to grasp — for, if this separate and immortal nature does exist, where is it and what is its nature? How does it contact and drive the body?

III

There is no possible way to know when men and women first began to consider that they were more than simply a physical form with life, that they had a spiritual quality and existence. Perhaps through dreams they realized that there was another self that existed, another self that could assume control while the body slept. And if this other self could function in some limited degree while the body slept, what could it do if it were completely free of bodily confinement?

No doubt sleepwalking was as occasional to prehistoric men and women as it is to moderns. To see a body fully asleep suddenly rise and begin walking must have been an astounding, fearful sight to the early cave dwellers — just as it still remains an incredibly interesting phenomenon to anyone who witnesses it today.

In societies that lived and worked by sunlight and retreated to hide and sleep at night there was plenty of time for reflection about men and nature. If man had this inner quality, or this *extra* quality, was it not possible that all things in nature had it just as well? The trees, the rivers, the animals?

But it this "self" which was so closely associated with mental activity, this thing which carried on through dreams while the body was in an unconscious state, was independent of, though connected to, the body, perhaps it lived on after death. Perhaps it just migrated from one bodily form to another, man to man, man to woman, or man to animal or plant and back again. Or, perhaps, when it was finally freed it became an invisible force knowing no limitation.

Gradually religions and cults developed which tried to explain the inner qualities of the soul, to see it as that part of every man and women with which the gods or God would deal after its physical trial on earth. With such perspective, and such teaching, men and women found ways in which to control the behavior of others; the weak were able to control the mighty. Foul play no matter how successful on earth would be dealt with by the gods, and one would do well to conform and love peace.

One might begin a survey of ancient ideas on immortality by turning back to 6th century Greece when there lived an itinerant teacher and philosopher by the name of Anaximenes. He imagined that the soul of every man or woman was very much like air. It could not actually be seen or touched but it could touch others and it could move others. And just as the air about us held together all things in the universe, so, too, did the soul hold together the human form.

Another ancient Greek philosopher, Heraclitus (535?-425 BC?) believed that an individual's soul was a special kind of fire, a kind of fire that was forever in a state of transition like all things in the universe. But it could never expire, this fire; it burned eternally. And as one fire could burn hotter than another, so too was one soul greater or lesser than another in goodness. Those souls which were closer to perfection he saw as having the hottest flame, a flame not unlike that which repesented the very essence of the universe.

Next come the ideas of Empedocles, who lived in Greece from 495-435 B.C. He argued that men do not only live in this physical world of which we are all aware. Men have another existence which goes far beyond the purely material. He wrote his ideas in a poem called *On the Nature of Things*. In it he emphasized his idea that just as the elements can never be corrupted, so man cannot be. There is a part of man which is eternal in nature.

Still another Greek philosopher, Democritus (460-370 BC), added new ideas about the soul. He, however, was strictly materialistic in his outlook. To him the world was made up of atoms so small that they could not be perceived by any of the senses. By their constant action and interaction they had created and now maintain the universe. The souls of men and women are likewise made of these atoms. When stored or assigned to human form, these soul-atoms become man or woman. With the corruption of the physical form which encases them, these atoms are freed to form again. They cannot be destroyed.

Now we meet again the ideas of Plato (427-347 BC), who believed it was impossible for anything which contained life to ever become non-living, just as it would be impossible for anything which did not contain life to become a living thing. To Plato, life itself was a principle. Souls, the elements of life, always exist. But they exist in their natural state in some far off abode until, for one reason or another, they desire the temporary advantages of a body. Then they are either sent to, or come on their own accord, to inhabit a world of material forms. If their lives on earth are successful, they return again to their usual state to bathe in the intellectual springs of a world filled with imagination and knowledge.

Plato held that the soul represents the simplest form that can possibly exist. There is absolutely nothing else which can be more simple in construction that the soul! Because of this, it is individable, indestructible. This same idea of simplicity, indivisibility, indestructibility has been carried on into Christian theology. But whereas Plato saw the soul as a material form, Christian theologians have envisioned it as a completely immaterial force.

Aristotle (384-322 BC) believed that the soul inhabited each and every form of life. Even plants have souls. However, the soul of man is the most sophisticated and possesses powers beyond that of mere plants and animals. But Aristotle never envisioned a personal immortality for the soul and saw it as one day being returned to final union with God.

The ideas of the Jewish Hellenistic philosopher, Philo Judaeus (2 BC - 40 AD) on the subject of immortality are much more complex. Philo believed that there are two types of souls, the *irrational* and the *rational*. The irrational souls are those which come into existence when the bodies of either men or women come into existence. The rational souls are those which came into being in the very beginning of creation; these have always existed and will always continue to exist with or without the human or animal forms in which they are contained or which they are tied to in some way. Rational souls may inhabit bodies already containing irrational souls. When these dual-souled bodies become corrupt — that is, they die — the irrational souls die but the rational souls live on. However, this continuing life of the rational souls continues only by permission of God, Who, at anytime, may bring their existence to an end.

To Epicurus (341-270 BC), the Athenian-born philosopher who established a community called the Garden, the soul is a physical thing, its composition being made up of countless atoms, though these are of the smallest kind. The atoms of the soul are not located in one single area of the body but are rather spread out through the entire body. All these soul-atoms are connected in some mysterious way to a soul-center, also located somewhere in the body, which controls all sensation. Because his ideas necessitated that the soul was a material substance, he could find no argument to justify immortality. Like all material substances, the soul would one day corrupt.

St. Augustine (354-430) also believed that man consisted of a soul and a body but he never saw the soul as simply material substance. In fact, he saw this union of body and soul in man to be a rather imperfect one. Only when the material body which forms about the soul finally dies does man begin to approach his perfect state. Augustine believed that men and their souls came into being at the same time. But the exact connection between the two, the exact way in which the soul drives the body, was a subject about which Augustine evidently cared little to speculate.

Backtracking now to Plotinus (205-270), we find that he had a somewhat different perspective than those before him. He expressed his ideas in the following way. Some souls, he wrote, take on material form, other souls remain immaterial. Those that do take on human form may enter hostile (terrestrial) or receptive (celestial) bodies. In its attempt to control the terrestrial body which it may inhabit, a soul may become so misdirected from its true purpose that it becomes thoroughly lost. To Plotinus, as you may remember from an earlier chapter, reincarnation was a very acceptable idea. He expressed, however, that this reincarnation in which he believed can be in the form of animal or plant life as well as human life. Thus, he would have us believe that the soul has an eternal quality, possibly taking on human or even animal form at times. The corruption of its physical state, however, in no way means that the soul itself has been corrupted.

One of the more famous Islamic philosophers, Avicenna (980-1037), argued that while the soul has no existence until the body is created, it lives on after the body dies. Avicenna also saw the body as little more than a vehicle with which the soul moves and communicates in its quest for eternal truth. When the vehicle no longer runs, the soul moves on. It cannot cease to exist because it is immaterial. Body is only its material form but *body is not soul.* Avicenna divided souls into two categories which he labeled perfect and imperfect. Those souls that lead physical existences but have not become slave to their physical passions are the perfect souls; they eventually pass on to a state of eternal bliss marked by complete freedom to pursue truth and knowledge. Those souls that live lives dedicated merely to the pursuit of physical satisfactions, thereby failing to reach their full potentials, pass into a state of continued torment; these are the imperfect souls.

Albert the Great (1200?-1280), a Doctor of the Roman Catholic Church, who wrote and taught science and natural philosophy as well as religion and theology, accepted the idea of Plato that the soul is substance and as such is immortal. Albert, however, sought to have us look at the relationship of body and soul in a different manner. Rather than to continue to perceive of the soul inhabiting and driving the body, he would have us see the body as simply the visible part of the soul; the body is, then, according to Albert, simply an extension of the soul. He saw the body as a necessary part of the soul because it gives the soul new dimension, new awareness — but he saw the body in no way to be necessary to the existence of the soul.

Marsilio Ficino (1433-1499), the Italian philosopher, brought together the arguments of Plato, Plotinus, Augustine, Averroes and Aquinas to make his own for the necessity of immortality. He saw the role of life as we know it as merely a means to finding truth; truth, ultimately, is God. He is the end toward which we all strive. If physical life means the end of the individual, then there can be no final and eternal union with God. Besides, Ficino, wrote, if man continually climbs toward a perfection, or degree of perfection, that can never be achieved because man is, in the final analysis, only mortal, then this is a contradiction, for it contradicts the idea we have of God as being all perfect and all good. Would a God who is all good bind men to a quest for that which can never be achieved?

On the opposite side of those who would seek philosophical

proof of immortality there was, for one, Cardinal Cajetan (Thomas de Vio), the Italian theologian and philosopher, who lived from 1468 to 1534. He claimed that there was no way to prove that the soul of man was immortal. The whole idea must be accepted on faith and faith alone! At least this was what he wrote and expressed publicly. Privately, he was more in accordance with the ideas of Avicenna, which is to say he saw the soul as an immaterial substance and, as such, had no need for dependence on the purely physical for survival. He believed any immaterial supernature must possess the attribute of immortality.

Juan Luis Vives (1492-1540), the Spanish humanist who was born in Valencia, and who was greatly influenced by the arguments of Augustine believed that it was the soul of man which was his driving force. But Vives felt that any efforts to try to determine just how the soul functions is completely out of place, well beyond the ability of man.

Giordano Bruno (1548-1600), who is still hailed as one of the greatest philosophers to emerge from the Renaissance, believed that the soul might be defined as a *monad,* which is a word derived from a Greek term meaning *unit.* Bruno believed that the soul-monad was similar in every way to the monads or basic elements which made up the entire universe. According to his theory, the soul must be a material form, not at all spiritual.

John Locke (1632-1716) saw the universe as consisting of two basic forms, one spiritual, the other physical. The soul, which is the spiritual form, is immaterial *yet* it is an intelligent entity. He saw the body and soul as interacting in the following way. The soul is the driving force of the body; it is that by which the body is able to move. As the body moves, it experiences; and by this experience of the body, the soul learns and forms ideas. Because it is immaterial in the first place, the soul may possibly continue to exist after bodily death, though to Locke this cannot be effectively argued and any hope of immortality must be relied on as faith rather than through reason.

Baruch Spinoza's ideas were similar to Cajetan's private feelings. In his *Ethics* (Part 5, Prop. 23), he explains that the human mind possess an eternal quality which allows it to exist after the body has died. He demonstrates this by explaining that in God there is a concept which expresses the very nature of human existence. "This conception or idea is therefore necessarily something which pertains to the essence of the human mind. But we ascribe to the human mind no duration which can be limited by time, unless in so far as it expresses the actual existence of the body, which is manifested through duration, and which can be limited by time; that is to say, we cannot ascribe duration to the mind except while the body exists. But, nevertheless, since this something is that which is conceived by a certain eternal necessity through the essence of God, this something which pertains to the essence of the mind will necessarily be eternal."

George Berkely (1685-1753), the Irish philosopher, saw mind and soul as synonymous terms. When we speak of the mind, we speak of the soul. To Berkely, real experience is only that which is experienced by the mind. It is infinite, can never die, and is of the same spiritual essence which ultimately defines the universe.

Gotfried Wilhelm Leibnitz (1646-1716) saw the soul in much the same way as Giordano Bruno, except Leibnitz stressed that the soul was a monad of a very special kind. Its quest is one for self-knowledge and what knowledge comes to it comes to it not from without, but from within. It is created with certain inherent characteristics and potential all of which may one day come to pass but not necessarily so. Much of its development or its realization of the knowledge it seeks will depend upon its experience in the world and the way in which it interprets that experience.

Immanual Kant (1724-1804) expressed in his *Critique of Practical Reason* (Chapter 2, part 4) that the immortality of the soul "is inseparably connected with the moral law." Kant was preoccupied with what he called the *summum bonum* (the highest good) and man's life in conjunction with it. It is in expressing his ideas on man's eternal reach for this highest good that Kant makes his comments about immortality.

"The realization of the *summum bonum* in the world is the necessary object of a will determinable by the moral law. But in this will the perfect accordance of the mind with the moral law is the supreme condition of the summum bonum. This, then, must be possible, as well as its object, since it is contained in the command to promote the latter. Now, the perfect accordance of the will with the moral law is holiness, a perfection of which no rational being of the sensible world is capable of at any moment of his existence. Since, nevertheless, it is required as practically necessary, it can only be found in a *progress in infinitum* towards that perfect accordance, and on the principles of pure practical reason, it is necessary to assume such a practical progress as the real object of our will.

"Now, this endless progress is only possible on the supposition of an *endless* duration of the *existence* and personality of the same rational being (which is called the immortality of the soul; consequently, this immortality, being inseparably connected with the moral law, is a postulate of pure practical reason (by which I mean a theoretical proposition) not demonstrable as such, but which is an inseparable result of an unconditional *a priori practical law.*"

William Paley (1743-1805) in Chapter 17 of his *Natural Theology,* that by no logic can we limit the properties of mind to any particular form or in any special area of space. He also explained that we cannot fall into the trap of overestimating the ability of our faculties; that is, we must never rely on the understanding that our five senses allow us to perceive all that there is to perceive.

Paley goes on to write that there are many in the animal kingdom that have only the senses of touch and taste; to them odors, sounds and colors do not exist. There are other animals that have an additional sense, that of smell. If these animals had the rational ability to reflect on their superiority over the two-sensed animals, could these of the extra sense rightly infer that they perceived all that was perceptible in nature? They might infer such a fallacy but we know that to others in nature there is the gift of hearing which brings to them a new class of awareness. Yet these animals have no sufficient ground to believe that by possessing all four known senses that they "comprehend all things and all properties of things which exist than might have been claimed by the tribes of animals beneath it. After all, we know that it is still possible to possess another sense, that of sight . . . This fifth sense makes the animal what the human animal is; but to infer that this fifth sense is the last sense, or that all five comprehend all existence is just as unwarrantable a conclusion as that which might have been made by any of the different species which possessed fewer. The conclusion of the one-sense animal and the five-sense animal stand upon the same authority." But, of course, there may be other senses, as the recent and more reputable research into psychic phenomena is beginning to reveal. There may very well be another world or other worlds beyond or beside ours but we have not yet evolved into the type of being that can sense them.

The Russian philosopher, Alexander Nikolayevich Radishchev (1749-1802) spent a good part of his life considering the possibility of immortality for man and he presented his ideas in a text titled: *On Man, His Mortality and Immortality,* published after his death in 1809. Radishchev argued that the soul was in no way dependent on the body and could not be corrupted at the time of bodily death.

In 19th century Germany, a physicist and philosopher named

Gustav Fechner (1801-1887) thought memory was in itself an argument for immortality of the soul. His argument goes something like this: In our everyday experiences we see and sense things that, while we are not immediately conscious of them, are tucked away in our memories. But though they were not consciously stored for later recall, they may at anytime be remembered. These memories never seem to vanish; they seem always to be in existence. Now just as memories exist in the minds of souls, so do souls exist in the mind of God, never to be lost, always to be remembered . . . always to exist.

John Stuart Mill (1806-1873), the English philosopher and economist, took a rather middle of the road approach to the subject of immortality. But this is not the result of any lack of investigation of the subject on his part. Mill is still a widely respected writer and philosopher and in the 19th century was, perhaps, the most influential philosopher in the entire world. Mill could find no sufficient argument to support the fact of immortality. But, on the other hand, he could find no sufficient argument against it. Thus, he saw no contradiction in taking the one stand or the other but inferred that, given the testimony offered through religious experience, there was certainly room for hope. Coming from a skeptic like Mill, such an attitude might be construed as a highly positive sign.

William James (1842-1910), the noted American philosopher and psychologist, in his *Principles of Psychology,* discussed (Chapter 10) the idea of the simplicity and substantiality of the soul; the very concept of it that we have seems to guarantee its reality. However, this immortality may not be the kind you or I might care to participate in. "The enjoyment of the atom-like simplicity of their substance in *saecula saeculorum* would not to most people seem a consumation devoutly to be wished." He goes on to write that "The demand for immortality is nowadays essentially theological. We believe ourselves immortal because we believe ourselves fit for immortality." In Chapter 21 he criticizes the belief in immortality once again when he writes: "The reason of the belief is undoubtedly the bodily commotion which it sets up: 'Nothing which I can feel like *that* can be false.' All our religious and supernatural beliefs are of this order. The surest warrant for immortality is the yearning of our bowels for our dear ones . . . "

In the 19th century there lived in England a psychical researcher who had dedicated his life to finding proof of the immortality of men and women. His name was Frederic Myers (1843-1901) and he had carved for himself a memorable career, first at Trinity College in Cambridge and then as an inspector of educational systems for the government. In his most noted work, *Human Personality and the Survival of Bodily Death,* he reported on a series of certainly unusual and mystical experiences which he felt proved the reality of immortality. He saw the spirit world as being governed by fundamental laws of science and through discovery of these laws we can track and communicate with the other world. He also felt that with or without a knowledge of these laws we might expect to make contact through some effort initiated from the spirit world.

The Scottish philosopher, Andrew Seth Pringle-Pattison (1856-1931) believed that immortality was possible but not guaranteed. He could not envision a good and perfect God bringing to eventual destruction that which He created and gave individual freedom. However, he could envision some selectivity on the part of God concerning to whom the privilege of immortality should be given.

The Islamic metaphysician, Muhammad Iqbal (1877-1938), believed in personal immortality. However, his views differed widely from many religious ideas that prevail today. That is, he did not see the purpose of the soul to be final and total union with God. Iqbal believed that the soul is created to be free and as it approaches ever closer (but not finally) to God, it becomes ever more free. While the soul is never completely unattached from God's existence, the soul is individual and will always remain individual. It comes to God in terms of perfection but not to Him in terms of submergence.

SUMMARY

Is there really such a thing as a soul?

Perhaps Aquinas answers the question once and for all when he explains that the soul is not a body but rather the first principle of life. It is the act of a body in the same way that the principle of heating is not a body but the act of a body. This thing which we refer to as the soul (or the mind or the intellect) operates apart from the body which it governs. It is the intrinsic or essential nature of that body which we recognize by physical form. The soul is the very *principle of life.*

Other philosophers have expressed their belief in the immortality of the soul but have differed somewhat on its fundamental nature or the right to immortal existence.

- Philo Judaeus believed there are two types of souls, one rational, the other irrational. Only the rational souls have the privilege of immortality.
- Plotinus believed that there are two different kinds of bodies a soul inhabits: hostile (terrestrial) and receptive (celestial). Hostile bodies might very well so complex the soul that the soul is led away from its true goals and thereby is lost to eternity.
- Avicenna wrote that the soul is created when the body comes into being. It has no pre-existence. The body is little more than a vehicle which the soul uses during its search for true meaning.
- Albert The Great believed that the body is irrelevant to the existence of the soul. He saw the body as a part of the soul rather than the soul as part of the body.
- Marsilio Ficino believed the soul is in a constant search for God and all the truth and beauty which is essential to His nature. The soul must be immortal for it cannot hope to reach God in the very short span of time that it has on earth.
- Cardinal Cajetan, however, could find no satisfactory philosophical proof for the immortality of the soul. He believed that immortality could only be accepted on faith, and faith alone.
- Baruch Spinoza argued that the human mind possesses an eternal quality which assures its immortality. He demonstrated his proof in his *Ethics.*
- Immanual Kant wrote that man could only achieve the highest good if there was at least one other existence after this one . . . "this immortality," he wrote, "is a postulate of pure practical reason . . . is an inseparable result of an unconditional *a priori* practical law."
- Alexander Nikolayevich Radishchev stressed that the soul's existence is in no way dependent upon the bodily form which is either resident in the body or governs it in some way. To Radishchev, the soul is incorruptible, which is to say it cannot be destroyed.
- Gustav Fechner wrote that the way we receive, either consciously or unconsciously, our memories indicate that these memories indeed never vanish. He explains that we are to God what our memories are to us. If God is eternal then so, too, must we be.

But where does the soul reside? No one really has the final answer. But the question will be considered with greater depth in Chapter 8.

CHAPTER 6
The Teleological Argument For Immortality

Perhaps the criticism by Ludwig Feuerbach (1804-1872) sums up man's quest for proof of immortality. In his *Thoughts Regarding Death and Immortality,* he wrote that the concept or hope of personal immortality was simply the ego of man revolting against the idea of his own final elimination.

All the arguments of the great philosophers who believed in an after-life, in the final analysis, simply adds up to so many paragraphs of well constructed arguments that can never be verified by experience. There just seems to be no scientific reason for the possibility of immortality.

Or is there? Empirical observation during the 1800's led scientists to a principle called *conservation of energy,* a principle which states that while energy can be transformed, it cannot be created or destroyed. Actually, energy exists in a number of forms including, for example, mechanical, thermal and chemical forms. There are two ways of describing energy and these are: as energy associated with motion (kinetic); as energy related simply to position (potential). When either of these energy forms are transformed either the kinetic or potential energy will be increased or decreased but the total of both the kinetic and potential sources will always remain the same.

The energy of the universe, then, exists always in the same measure though it may at anytime move from one state to another. If this is a universal pattern, it is not so outlandish to apply the same principle to the life of the soul — that is, to see the soul as a forever existing substance which at one time or another may be transformed from an immaterial to a material state but which can never be destroyed.

To add force to this argument, let's consider the very elements found listed in any chemistry book. These elements, in their individual states, or through combination with one or more other elements, bring into form the matter with which we exist or coexist. These elements appear to be incorruptible. They exist. They just simply exist. What final form they may construct or be constructed to depends upon the chemical relationships in which they play a part. But whatever is the final physical form they construct, once these forms corrupt, the elements continue to exist, not in lesser or greater degree. These elements are called elements because they are *elementary* — changeless, indestructibly basic, and therefore necessary. If there are basic indestructible elements in the universal scheme of things, why cannot the human personality (or individuality) have a fundamental element, which we will call the soul, at its core.

The idea of an unchanging quantity of universal energy and elements which are incorruptible is no definite scientific argument for the personal immortality of the human soul but it does at least acknowledge that there are what seems to be eternal elements in the universe. Whether or not this idea of incorruptibility can be carried from the material to the immaterial world (where the soul originates) is another question. But it is at least important to realize that in our time, in our universe, the idea of eternalness is by no means strange.

Now, probably the closest one can come to giving scientific basis to any philosophical argument about the existence of the soul (or of God, for that matter) is to construct teleological proofs. Teleology looks for goal-directed activity in the things we feel, see or sense in the physical world.

Thus there is a special magic to teleological arguments. They bring philosophy onto a plain which is easily comprehended by the average man or woman. For once, philosophers are functioning in the world of reality instead of pure thought. Teleological arguments are concerned with design, activity and function, subjects which are at least *sensible*.

There are some abstract things which exist in the human mind which we cannot touch or photograph but can at least identify from the results which they effect. There is no physical tie, of course, but there is, nonetheless, a direct relationship.

We know, for instance, that men and women engage in intellectual activity; we know that by their skill in those areas of mathematics which require more than memorization. We know that men and women have a spiritual quality for they are capable of self-sacrifice for a higher good regardless of the extent of the physical, economical, social or political consequence. We know that they have creative ability, also, and we recognize this through their art and music, if through nothing else. But we cannot photograph, touch, feel, smell, hear or in any way sense the intellect, the spirit, the creative force. Yet we know these all exist. We know them by results that can be attributed to their existence.

And we all know that as we grow older — and in doing so, observe more, study more, and as we inevitably begin to rely less and less on our physical prowess: use our heads more — these intellectual, spiritual and creative abilities tend to sharpen. Sometimes they are dulled by lack of activity or disease. But this dullness is never due to a disease of the intellect, the spirit or the creative force, but due to a disease which effects the vehicle by which these forces operate in the sensible world: the body.

In our society we tend to put breaks on the spirit that guides the intellect and the creative force. This point is probably best illustrated by the executive in a corporation who worked hard all his life to develop the knowledge, sophistication and political sense to make it to the top of his organization and to guide that organization efficiently. Then at age 65 he is forced into retirement.

He is physically worn and his appearance shows age. His hair is gray, he may be a little stooped; he hasn't the physical power he once had, but he is smarter, more ethical, more patient, more informed, more capable than he has ever been to lead others. Yet, retirement! He is forced to retire when he has more than he has ever had to give, when he has so much more yet to grow before he can reach his full potential in those eternal qualities that seem to exist apart from his physical body.

This same perplexity appears at the end of any rational man or woman's life. Suddenly their time is up but there is so much more they want to do, can do (although there are things they can no longer do). At death he or she feels so deprived. Death seems to come as a thief ready to deprive its victim of fulfilling all his or her potential. But, in actuality, death only comes to relieve a person of further pain or discomfort associated with physical deterioration.

II

Immanual Kant treats this same idea in his *Critique of Pure Reason*[1] where he discusses the idea of the existence of God. He writes there that teleological unity is an important consideration in his own concept of nature because there appears to be such overwhelming evidence of it. It leads him "to the assumption that a supreme intelligence has ordered all things according to wisest ends." Kant later adds that, "In the wisdom of a Supreme Being, and in the shortness of life, so inadequate to the development of the glorious powers of human nature, we may find equally sufficient grounds for a doctrinal belief in the human soul."

But what if there is no God? Kant goes on to explain that the reality of a moral belief which guides mankind confirms the conclusions he draws from his teleological observations. The end for which the moral order must be meant confirms "the existence of God and of a future world."[2] Kant admits that his convictions are not logical but rather moral and therefore rest on purely subjective grounds. " . . . . and since it rests on moral grounds," he explains, "I must not even say *it is* morally certain that there is a God, etc., but that *I am* morally certain; that is, my belief in God and in another world is so interwoven with my moral nature that I am under as little apprehension of having the former torn from me as losing the other."

Kant saw death not as an end but simply as a phase of transition, very possibly, perhaps, a step toward a dimension in which all further potential of those special human qualities of which we have spoken, can be realized. Other philosophers have echoed Kant's thoughts. In this life there is no possible way men and women can realize all of their potential and realize them to the n'th degree. If there is a perfect God it seems calculable that He would create a perfect system in which all of one's potential can be realized.

Some see that other world as "Heaven." Others see it in terms of reincarnation. Others see it in terms of a spiritual existence which moves continually about the universe, taking on physical form where and whenever it so wishes or is to directed.

Exactly how this next existence is affected or where it occurs —well, these are subjects for debate. But the probability of a future existence, given the idea of a perfect God and teleological necessity, is quite high, indeed.

III

In summary: Man would like to find a scientific proof of what he feels is his immortal nature. If he can discover physical laws which indicate that things in this universe go on without interruption, though they may be transformed from one state to another, then there is always the possibility that he, too, has the chance of a future existence — and has possibly had, for that matter, a past existence.

Whether or not a truly scientific proof is possible remains arguable. Clearly, there are some things we are meant to know with little certainty. Through science we can discover a great deal about what happens in the universe, but science can never reveal to us exactly why it happens. The big "why" in all of life is left to religious faith, and religion requires no logical order for it functions in a "theater" of awareness that requires no rational analysis. But from science's investigations, we have developed a teleology that helps us transcend the separate levels on which religions and science operate.

Most of the teleological arguments for immortality grasp at the idea that men and women are in continuing growth toward their full potential. But no man or woman can ever come close to realizing their full potential here on earth, for physical death prevents them from the endless time they may need.

As Immanual Kant put it: "In the wisdom of the Supreme Being, and in the shortness of life, so inadequate to the development of the glorious powers of human nature, we may find . . . sufficient grounds for a doctrinal belief in the future life of the human soul.

CHAPTER 7
On Life and Death and Good and Evil

One cannot become involved in a discussion on the immortality of the soul without some words spent on the purpose of life and death, for the qeustion that sooner or later comes to mind is: "Why the need for a temporary physical state in the immortal or eternal life of the soul."

After all, if the soul is immaterial and exists with or without its animal form, why the necessity for it to spend life as we know life. It stands to reason that there must be a purpose for this transitional period in the life of the soul. There must be a divine scheme behind it all, many feel, and they've searched the physical and metaphysical sciences to find the purpose of life. But, at the same time, many great minds have rejected the idea of a cosmic scheme and have argued that all of life is, in the final analysis, worthless. It is worthless, they feel, because it has no meaning beyond the present, and all of life will one day, no doubt, come to an end.

But most things in the world are not worthless. Most things have a purpose and function for a higher cause. Why not life?

One of the great philosophers who preferred the negative view toward all of existence was Bertrand Russell (1872-1970), the noted British philosopher and mathematician. Russell pointed out that there is no evidence available to substantiate that what we identify as mental life can continue when the brain and the nervous system die. He admits, of course, that this is only an argument based on a lack of proof and as such is relatively weak. But, he insisted, as weak as the argument is, it stands with greater strength than those arguments which are offered to contradict it.

Arthur Schopenhauer (1788-1860), the noted German philosopher, had similar ideas. He wrote that there is no evidence of real meaning in life and if he were personally given the choice he would find no reason to accept it for himself. (But, of course, in having been given the choice, he must have had some other existence in which to reject or accept it). According to Schopenhauer, happiness is there to always be strived for but never, never to be realized.

Many other philosophers and writers also underscored the pain and sorrow which must be endured in every life, that pain and sorrow only to be culminated when the life that experiences it is itself culminated.

The arguments put forth by the pessimists such as Russell and Schopenhauer and others are not so easily put aside. They make their points well and we, all of us, have shared some of the misery of every other man or woman — at least to some degree — either through our own circumstance or through the sickness, accident or death that has come to our own loved ones. But it is necessary to note that if men like Russell and Schopenhauer believed that all of life was of no meaning, why then did they work as exhaustingly as they did to present their ideas? Wouldn't they have envisioned all that they did to be in vain? If life has no meaning, then what meaning could they expect from their extensive efforts and dedication to convince all of us of our useless existence?

Nonetheless, when we look at war, sickness, physical defects, the hate that encompasses the world, this certainly does appear to be, at times, a life of evil rather than of goodness. But in many cases the evil that comes to men and women can be traced to mankind's own ignorance and/or greed, to man's inhumanity to man. Injustice, social and economic misery stem from the systems of man and his relationships; these are not weapons or designs of God.

To this many would be quick to respond that it is true these things are not the doing of God but are to be traced to man's inconsiderations — but what about disease, and storm, and flood, and all the other catastrophe that exists in the natural world? These are not brought about by men and women and their unleashed greed and passion but by forces beyond their control.

This point is, of course, well taken, for there are indeed systems of "evil" which are at the present time beyond the control of men and women. But when one investigates this subject in relation to the special freedom which mankind enjoys, the special purposes of the design we find in nature, and the fundamental causes of evil, one's perspective begins to change.

There probably is no natural "evil." There is nature and the way it is worked (*not* the way it works, for nature does nothing but is rather *done to* or *with*.) Very often men and women get in the way of its workings and thus suffer. But as science progresses and nature is further understood, these things which are interpreted as "evil" may very well be found to be necessities which man can one day use to his own advantage.

But for a satisfactory perspective of "evil" in nature, let us first consider the special freedom that men and women enjoy, a freedom which is above and beyond that which other creatures in the universe are afforded.

All other animals are restrained or governed by their instincts and their environment. This is to say that the gorilla, the elephant, the tiger, is *tied* to this world of natural phenomena. They perform on instinct and instinct alone. Their intellect is "hardwired" to a great percent. They are a part of the world, are dependent upon it, and will never rise above it.

Men and women have not the same natural constraints as do animals. They have their "hardwired" instincts to be sure, but they can at anytime work to rise above them. Aquinas explains this special freedom in terms of man's reason and free will. In his *Summa Theologica* (Part 1, Section 2, Quest. 1, Art. 1) he writes as follows: " . . . man differs from irrational creatures in this, that he is a master of his actions . . . Now man is master of his actions through his reason and will; hence, too, free choice is called *the power of will and reason*. Therefore those actions are properly called human which proceed from a deliberate will."

Men and women certainly seem to have been given a certain kind of freedom, or else have earned it. God, if He exists, seems to have no desire to infringe on that freedom or respects it to such an ultimate degree that He would have no thought about inhibiting it unless it would result in some greater good for Him to do so. Freedom seems to be a natural attribute of the human condition, a natural attribute of the human soul. Rather than to restrict men and women and make them spiritual robots it would appear that God wishes them to be free spirits in every sense of the idea which the term "free spirit" designates.

One might say that *Nature* has provided man with the basic instincts to carry him forth in the world until he can lead his own way by appropriate use of his intellect and physical abilities. That is, we would ordinarily say *Nature* except that *Nature* does nothing but is rather *done to.* Something directs Nature — we must at least admit this — and this awesome director we call God.

Today we witness horrible deaths by cancer and other diseases. And in times gone by men and women have met horrible torture and death at the hands of other men. But in the natural order of things, death has special meaning, as you will see later in this chapter, and ordinarily does not come with the awful torment and degradation that we witness. Cancer and many of the diseases we observe with fright are, in the final analysis, brought upon man by man himself, by the chemicals he uses before he understands their effect, by the things he does to his food and water before he has finally investigated the consequences that would result. God through nature takes time. Man was not just thrust upon the world but millions of years of development first took place — everything carefully planned and made ready — before he was allowed to be. But man moves with awful and careless speed, though much less so today than before thanks to environmentalists and others who stand ready to cry out and demonstrate until the studies are begun to ascertain what repercussions may result.

In any of the awful occurrences that we witness today, which bring men and women quickly to the ends of their lives on earth, if God were to personally intervene He would infringe upon that special freedom given every man and every woman. And as they came to depend upon Him for guidance through every difficulty, they would not grow toward their true potential but would become as sheep ever dependent upon the shepherd. Clearly it appears that the last God wants of humankind is that they become sheep. He wants men and women to reach for the stars and beyond, to reach for Him, who Kant describes as the highest good. But if He is indeed an all-perfect, all-powerful God as He is perceived, He would want to be worshipped as the highest good not out of vanity but out of generosity; that is, in reaching for the highest good every man and women comes closer to their own full potential and to what is best for them.

II

William Paley (1743-1805), the English theologian and moral philosopher, who is remembered best for his *Natural Theology,* in which he formulates a teleological proof for the existence of God, tackles the subject of pain, death and evil in the world in very simplistic but effective terms.

In an earlier work titled *Moral and Political Philosophy,* he wrote[1] as follows:

"When God created the human species either he wished their happiness, or he wished their misery, or he was indifferent and unconcerned about either.

"If he had wished our misery, he might have made sure of his purpose, by forming our senses to be so many sores and pains to us, as they are now instruments of gratification and enjoyment; or by placing us amidst objects so ill-suited to our perceptions as to have

69

continually offended us, instead of ministering to our refreshment and delight. he might have made, for example, everthing we tasted bitter; everything we saw loathsome; everything we touched a sting; every smell a stench; and every sound a discord.

"If he had been indifferent about our happiness or misery, we must impute to our good fortune (as all design by this supposition is excluded) both the capacity of our senses to receive pleasure, and the supply of external objects fitted to produce it.

"But either of these, and still more both of them, being too much to be attributed to accident, nothing remains but the first supposition, that God, when he created the human species, wished their happiness; and made for them the provision which he has made, with that view and for that purpose.

"The same argument may be proposed in different terms, thus: Contrivance proves design; and the predominate tendency of the contrivance indicates the disposition of the designer. The world abounds with contrivances; and all the contrivances which we are acquainted with, are directed to beneficial purposes. Evil no doubt exists; but it is never, that we can perceive, the object of contrivance. Teeth are contrived to eat, not to a ache; their aching now and then is incidental to the contrivance, perhaps inseparable from it: or, even if you will, let it be called a defect in the contrivance; but it is not the object of it. This is a distinction which well deserves to be attended to. In describing implements of husbandry, you would hardly say of the sickle, that it is made to cut the reaper's hand, though, from the construction of the instrument, and the manner of using it, the mischief often follows. But if you had occasion to describe instruments of torture or execution, this engine, you would say, is to extend the sinews; this to dislocate the joints; this to break the bones; this to scorch the soles of the feet. Here pain and misery are the very objects of the contrivance. Now, nothing of this sort is to be found in the works of nature. We never discover a train of contrivance to bring about an evil purpose. No anatomist ever discovered a system of organization, calculated to produce pain and disease; or, in explaining the parts of the human body, ever said, this is to irritate; this is in inflame; this duct is to convey the gravel to the kidneys; this gland to secrete the humour which forms the gout. And if by chance he came at a part of which he does not know the use, the most he can say is, that it is useless; no one ever suspects that it is put there to incommode, to annoy, or to torment."

What point Paley argues well is that there is no sign of things contrived for the purpose of evil, no matter where we look. If there is evil it is by accident. God, if He exists, does not will evil or design anything for the purpose of effecting it.

Thus if those nihilist philosophers like Schopenhauer and Russell want to point to the pain and misery in the world, they can no way prove that these occur by the will of God.

III

Aquinas tackles the subject of evil[2] in greater depth. In explaining the cause of it he writes that it is,

" ... the absence of the good which is natural and due a thing ... evil has no formal cause, rather it is a privation of form; likewise, neither has it a final cause, but rather is it a privation of order and to the proper end, since not only the end has the nature of good, but also the useful, which is ordered to the end. Evil, however, has a cause by way of an agent, not per se, but accidently."

" ... in proof of this, we must know that evil is caused in the action otherwise than in the effect. In the action evil is caused by reason of the defect of some principle of action, either of the principle or the instrumental agent; thus the defect in the movement of an animal may happen by reason of the weakness of the motive power, as in the case of children, or by reason of the ineptitude of the instrument, as in the lame. On the other hand, evil is caused in a thing, but not in the proper effect of the agent or of the matter. It is caused by reason of the power or perfection of the agent when there necessarily follows on the form intended by the agent the privation of another form; as, for instance, when on the form of fire there follows the privation of the form of air or of water. Therefore, as the more perfect the fire is in strength, so much the more perfectly does it impress its own form, so also does it more perfectly corrupt the contrary. Hence that evil and corruption befall air and water comes from the perfection of the fire; but this is accidental, because fire does not aim at the privation of the form of water, but at the bringing in at its own form, though in doing this it accidently causes the other. But if there is a defect in the proper effect of the fire — as, for instance, that it fails to heat — this comes either by defect of the action, which implies the defect of some principle, as was said

71

above, or by the indisposition of the matter, which does not receive the action of fire acting on it. But this very fact that it is a deficient being is accidental to good to which of itself it pertains to act. Hence it is true that evil in no way has any but an accidental cause; and thus is good and the cause of evil."

We might translate this into a slightly more practical example. Fire is evil when we do not understand it and cannot control it. It was evil to prehistoric man until he learned to use it for his own aims and came to understand under what conditions it could be for the bad and could be for the good. Similarly, much of the evil we see in the world is simply the accidental cause of that which we have not yet come to understand and control. In the relationships among men and women, however, there is indeed evil intent. Contrived evil belongs in the affairs of men not of God.

Would God at any time cause evil?

Aquinas answers,[4] " . . . the evil which consists in the defect of action is always caused by the defect of the agent. But in God there is no defect, but the highest perfection. Hence, the evil which consists in defect of action, or which is caused by defect of agent, is not reduced to God as to its cause."

But now, what about the purpose of life? What can that purpose be?

Assuming that life is not the result of some cosmic accident, this assumption being made on the weight of the various teleological arguments, one must assume that, if there is a God, life exists because He so wills it. That there is a God can be believed on the weight of philosophical and certain religious arguments which, though they are not all conclusive, are sufficiently more weighty than the arguments against His (or Her) existence. Why He should will that others live also has always been an intriguing subject.

Much of the philosophy on the subject argues that we are, in life, graduating toward a complete unison with God. Some religions have accepted this as meaning that we will one day be completely reabsorbed into the mind of God where we had first originated. But this is not necessarily what is meant by final communion with God as, perhaps, both Euckin and Teilhard De Chardin clearly illustrate for us.

IV

The German philosopher, Rudolph Christoph Euckin (1846-1926), expressed that while the human soul had its beginning in the natural world, it has the potential of transcending it. His ideas are not dissimilar to Aquinas'. However, Euckin puts his philosophy on the following terms. The purpose of each individual life is to finally attain the ultimate truth and beauty of person, at which time the individual life will become bound with God as well as with each and every other life. But it will not become so bound in its ultimate state that it would lose all of its individual freedom. Rather, in reaching this ultimate state it will achieve complete freedom but not freedom from truth and goodness which every other life will also achieve, this truth and goodness being necessary attributes of God.

Thus, as Euckin might explain it, the purpose of human life is to bring into existence the human soul. And its physical life is meant to be a search for the ultimate qualities that, when achieved, will make it one with God.

Euckin's ideas have been expressed also by other philosophers, most recently by Pierre Teilhard De Chardin (1881-1955), the French priest (Roman Catholic) and paleoanthropologist. He has written that the purpose of life is to bring man ever closer to the same type of freedom and perfection that God Himself enjoys. To Teilhard, it is not inconceivable that God's ultimate plan is to share all of eternity with beings exactly like Himself.

But if it is the goal of every human soul to obtain its full potential as a free and perfect being, what about death which deprives every individual of reaching his or her full potential?

Well, we do not know that death deprives the individual of reaching his or her full potential. All that we know is that death deprives the individual of its material existence here on Earth. If we accept the idea of the immortality of the individual personality, then death is no more than a transitional phase in which the soul continues on its way to another dimension of experience and awareness.

But why must there be death? Why cannot the all-perfect Creator bring forth unending life?

"Immortality upon this earth is out of the question," William Paley would tell us[5], "Without death there could be no generation, no sexes, no parental relation, i.e., as things are constructed, no animal happiness."

V

In summary:

If the soul is immortal and can exist with or without the body, why the need for a temporary physical existence?

Perhaps, some of the more direct answers to this question come to us from the writings of Euckin, Aquinas and Avicenna and other philosophers who have argued that the soul is created when the body is created. The soul takes on the physical form by which we know it as a necessary stage in its ascendance toward God.

Many philosophers, however, have preferred to take a rather negative attitude about life and its purpose. They have looked at the misery constant in the world and have perceived life as evil rather than good.

But evil is by accident and good by contrivance in the natural world of things, as William Paley has pointed out. As he explained it, when God created human life He either wanted it to experience happiness or misery, or He was completely indifferent and unconcerned about either.

If He wished our misery, He could have made sure of His purpose by so designing our senses that they would bring us little but annoyance and pain. The tooth would not be in place to allow us to eat but rather to ache whenever we attempted to chew.

If He were indifferent, at the time of our creation, about our happiness and misery, we would not be able to find so many things in nature designed for the good. In fact, wherever we look there we find not purposeful evil but purposeful good — that is, in everything except the affairs of men.

"Evil no doubt exists," Paley wrote, "but is never, that we can perceive, the object of contrivance. Teeth are constructed to eat, not to ache, their aching now and then is incidental to the contrivance, perhaps inseparable from it: or even, if you will, let it be called a defect in the contrivance; but it is not the object of it . . . "

If whenever one sees contrivance he sees a good to be effected, he can very well be assured that where he sees life only good is to be effected. But lives go bad. Does this mean that God designed these lives to follow such negative paths?

Aquinas answered this last question by stating that evil occurs when the agent of that evil is defective. In God, however, there is no defect only the highest perfection. Thus any evil is not the result of action by God but by the agent of the cause which brings about the evil.

Now, on the question of the purpose of life: Is it only for the reasons that Euckin and others have expressed: the means by which souls are created?

If certainly cannot be for God — if he is all powerful — can just as well create the soul by other means. Therefore, life as we know it must have some divine purpose, of that we can be sure. It plays its part in the necessary development of the soul but is not necessary to the existence of the soul (remember Socrates' argument). Exactly what part it plays may be obvious when we look at the teleological arguments which point to the every increasing value of the human personality as it matures with age.

CHAPTER 8
The Spiritual Connection

One of the many great questions that still plagues philosophers concerns exactly what may be the spiritiual-to-physical connection between soul and body. Regardless of whether the soul is located within or without the body, in some way it must be able to control the body, in order to summon specific thoughts, analyze, theorize, guide, decide, search for the highest good.

Descartes took a stab at the problem but was never able to sufficiently defend his explanation. After doing some research into the latest findings in human anatomy he became convinced that a small reddish-gray cone of matter attached at the base of the brain was the office of the soul. What he had zeroed in on is something called the pineal gland, which, even today, remains somewhat of a mystery as no one is quite sure of what part it plays — or once played in the early stages of evolution. Descartes was under the mistaken notion that the gland was peculiar only to humans and did not exist in other animals.[1] But the fact is that the pineal gland is found in all verterbrates.[2]

If indeed the soul, or its medium, were situated in the skull and attached to the base of the brain, a great many philosophers and theologians will be greatly surprised. After all, the soul is considered a spiritual thing independent of the physical world. Should men of science and medicine stumble upon the physical side of the spiritual connection, then science, in its continuing probe for natural knowledge, will have stumbled upon a discovery never again to be surpassed.

In science, and even in philosophy, there remains a tendency to seek the material form of that which is generally held to be immaterial. Even an explanation like that of William James', which defines the mind simply as a *stream of consciousness,* brings to it a physical description, for where there is consciousness there are a series of detectable electrical and chemical actions. And because any mental activity requires such stimulus of the brain, mental activity in itself cannot be indicative of *soul.*

But suppose that one *does* accept the possibility of a material location within the brain through which the soul communicates to the body. If he or she can accept that, well, they should just as well be able to accept that the entire body is a physical representation of the soul, that the body is simply the form of the soul here on earth — or, more exactly, the body is the physical means by which the soul expresses itself on this planet.

The soul may very well be *one with* the body but at the same time able to transcend it. As long as the body exists, the soul remains with it. One may, in fact, speculate that it can leave the body at anytime, however its first or subsequent assignment to physical form is not its own; it may be required to remain as long as the body continues to exist. Upon physical death it may find some type of freedom until reassignment (to Heaven, hell, purgatory, limbo, another body — to *where* is not relevant here) unless there is a privilege to be granted to it allowing it to take on physical form at will, effecting its own incarnations; and such privilege, one might surmise, may be its final reward.

But why would an immaterial life, existing under no limitation, suddenly choose to submit itself for the first time, or again, to all the limitations that a physical body would inflict upon it? The answer may be that physical extension brings new dimension to the existence of spiritual beings, a *new* or *additional* way in which spiritual forms can be in contact with, communicate with, enjoy, other souls. After all, spiritual joys may be the highest, but spiritual life cannot be *every-thing,* for how can something be *everything* when it is lacking some capabilities; and spiritual existence lacks physical form and related sensation although it does not require either.

Where is the mind (or soul, or psyche)?

For thousands of years it was assumed that, if it existed at all, it was located somewhere in the brain. But, today, as neuroscientists probe the cerebral cortex, which is the area from which the more complex mental functions occur, they find no sign of anything which is the source for its direction and performance. What they find rather are complex chemical and electrical forces interacting in such a way as to account for the human phenomenon. Whatever it is that may cause the brain to seek the highest good even by sacrificing its own satisfactions may simply be contained in the inherent structure of this complex "computer."

Lacking physical proof of a soul, scientists infer that if there is something called a mind it has to be created when the brain reaches a certain level of sophistication, so that the word itself comes to describe not an entity independent of the natural machine it operates but rather a level of maturity in the cognitive abilities of the machine itself. But, then again, these pathfinders of neuroscience are searching for a physical substance when, in fact, what they need do is transcend the physical to the spiritual. As deeply as they cut into the depths of the brain, as far as they may search into its complexity, they can never go beyond the limits of sensibility. To paraphrase Kant, in searching for the soul they are searching for a part of the ultimate reality to which it belongs. But if the ultimate reality transcends the natural world, how is science to take the leap from the material world into the immaterial? How can it possess the tools to do so? The objective of science is knowledge of nature and the physical world. The soul cannot be a part of the physical world if it is spiritual.

Individuals generally associate the soul with the mind or give it some home within the parameters of the human form. Some more enlightened theorists tend to see the body as belonging to the soul or simply being its physical representation. There is always a tendency to give a relative location for something unexplainable and a double tendency to forget that this assignment was simply relative, simply theoretical. The quickest example with which everyone can identify is the assignment of heaven and hell, should they exist. Heaven is up, hell is down. Up where? Down where? If we can return in our thoughts, for but a moment, to a picture of our galaxy floating through eternal space, where both an individual standing on the Earth's northern polar region and another standing on the southern must look up to see the sky but different stars, up and down are completely relative terms.

If the soul is spiritual, strictly immaterial, it need not be contained in the body. It can very well exist without the body or envelope the entire body. In this last case the body may simply be the physical part of the soul. The soul of a six foot man may be twelve feet, to give an absurd but clarifying example, or it may be as all encompassing as the air. That is, as the wind is the really sensible part of the air, the body is the sensible part of the soul.

Examples are never sufficient in dealing with spiritual subjects for when we move into the area of metaphysics we need to have a whole brand new set of categories and a completely new language with which to define them — as Augustine once pointed out and, more recently, Wittgenstein.

The question of whether the soul is in the body or the body is in the soul is one to be approached simply for the sake of argument. The question cannot be resolved and may not even be relevant when one considers the approach of Aquinas and Aristotle (to be given later in this chapter). In any event, piercing the brain with probes will admittedly bring one closer to a deeper understanding of the natural workings of the soul, but it will never bring anyone *to* the soul.

But one being contained in the other is not the only option. If spirit and body are connected in some divine way, the very nature of that which is spiritual would allow no limitation as to the distance of the soul from the body. It is quite conceivable that the soul may be a foot distant from the body through which it expresses itself, or a yard, or, for that matter, a mile or more. In our own highly limited physical existence we are able to control massive machines by remote devices, and we are only in our infancy in this technology; within the spiritual order of things it is not inconceivable, then, that another type of remote control, or attachment, is the norm.

The remarkable way in which we feel attached to every area of our bodies, however, gives little incentive for us to assume that the *basic us* (that is, the *mind* or *soul* — or body, if you will) can be both within and without the body at the same time — that is, be separate from it and yet guiding the body. But in our analogy of the car and driver to the body and soul, think how we may feel the vibrations of the car, the starting and stopping, the turning and the sudden impact during collision. Or consider the dirt-biker cross-countrying on his two-wheeler; he is certainly a part of that machine by the time he gets to San Francisco from New York. But he may leave that bike at anytime and carry away with him and use to even higher advantage all sensual perception that must have been, by necessity, limited to control of that machine.

This is all conjecture, of course, but put forth only to carry the argument that if the soul is immaterial — spiritual — it is by no means limited to any specific physical area. To think that it sits in the recesses of the brain where it serves as the core for all mental activity is to give it a physical office. It is more like the transparent but ever present air which is felt only through its body, the wind.

II

Aquinas investigated the subject of the soul on purely philosophical grounds. What is it? he asked. Is it corruptible? Is it subsistant?

Aquinas wrote that in order to discover exactly what is the nature of the soul, one must first accept it as being the first principle of life. Life is recognized as having knowledge and movement, although there are those who believe that only corporeal things can have knowledge and movement and that what does not exist as a body just does not exist.

"It is manifest," Aquinas wrote, "that not every principle of vital action is a soul, for then the eye would be a soul, as it is a principle of vision; and the same consideration might be applied to the other instruments of the soul; but it is the first principle of life that we call the soul."[3]

Aquinas continues to explain that though it may very well be that a body is a principle of life, as the heart of a creature is the principle of its life, *no body can be the first principle of life*. This is because to be a principle of life "does not pertain to a body as such since, then, every body (including a stone) would be a living thing, or a principle of life. Therefore a body is capable of being a living thing, or of being a principle of life, because it is this kind of body. Now the fact that it actually is such a kind of body is owed to some principle which is called *its act*. Therefore the soul, the first principle of life is not a body but the act of a body; just as heat, which is the principle of heating, is not a body but an act of a body."[4]

Aquinas goes on to write that the principle of intellectual operation called the soul is a principle which is at the same time "incorporeal and subsistant. For it is clear that by his intellect man can know the nature of all corporeal things. Now whatever knows certain things cannot have any of them in its own nature because that which is in it would naturally impede the knowledge of anything else."[5]

To illustrate this last point, Aquinas gives the example of the sick man whose tongue, rendered tasteless or foul-tasting by fever, cannot sense anything which is sweet; as a matter of fact, everything is bitter to that tongue. "Therefore, if the intellectual principle contained the nature of any body it would be unable to know all bodies. Now every body possesses its own determinate nature. Thus, it is not possible for the intellectual principle to be a body. It is also impossible for it to understand through a bodily organ since the determinate nature of the organ would impede knowledge of all bodies — as when a certain color is not only in the pupil of the eye but in a glass vase as well — and the liquid in the vase appears to be the same color."[6]

Thus, Aquinas goes on to point out, that governing force that we refer to as the mind, or the intellect, or the psyche, or the soul, operates apart from the body which it governs. It is the intrinsic or essential nature of the thing we recognize simply by its physical form. Now only that which has its own existence can operate apart from the body. There is nothing we know of that can operate except a being in act, "hence a thing operates according as it is. For this reason we do not say that heat imparts heat but that which is hot gives heat. We must conclude, therefore, that the human soul which is known as the intellect or the mind, is something incorporeal and subsistent."[7]

Aquinas, as one can readily observe, though a religious individual, and particularly a devout Catholic, never thought to simply use faith as an argument for the existence of the soul. He sought to establish strong philosophical foundations for his theology and his religious practice. Aquinas was not simply a Doctor of the Church but also a philosopher of the highest order and he followed the example set by many philosophers before him who not only sensed the existence of the soul but sought to find proof of it.

III

But to assume that the soul itself needs to affect the electrical and chemical stimulus of a brain in order to effect mental processes seems to be a bit contradictory. Think for the moment of our general idea of God as someone who transcends the world of corruptible materialism, who is spiritual and, just as well, an intelligence, and an intelligence of the highest order. That is, there is no intelligence which is greater than God's. In this impression that we harbor of Him, we see him as wholly spiritual, beyond the mere physical (though we allow that at will he can become material). Yet we admit that this intricately designed world of ours, the solar system in which it sits, and the galaxy in which this solar system fits, are all owing to His unlimited knowledge, wisdom and goodness. We give Him knowledge and wisdom but still subscribe to the idea that He requires no physical brain, no physical body whatever. Yet without this body we assume He can see and hear, feel and communicate, effect and react. Now, we assign the soul to the same spiritual state which God inhabits, yet we insist the soul needs the electrical and chemical stimulus of a brain with which to think, needs that spongy three or four pound computer underneath our skulls.

The dilemma here is that if the soul does not need the brain in order to think, why the measurable mental activity everytime a person contemplates a decision? One understands why the body needs the brain for its motor activities, for its reflexes and all animal-level survival commands, but why, then, would those higher mental activities, which some say are indicative of soul, necessitate brain activity?

The answer may be that the body, the physical image of the soul, the physical duplicate, perhaps, needs the brain; not the soul. In the spiritual community the very same thought processes are carried on by the soul without use of this three pound computer, much as God is able to carry on — if it is true — his universal existence and activity without any physical requirement.

The point that is being led to here, or, rather, one speculation that is being presented about this spiritual connection, is that the soul and the body are *one.* Do not look for the valve that allows the spiritual signals to flow to the physical body much like the valves of the heart open and close to assure the blood moves in the right direction. The soul and the body may just very well be one and the same.

But does this indicate that there is *only* physical existence and men and women are mortal? No, it does not.

What is necessary here is an example that will illustrate how the body and soul can be one and yet allow that the soul transcends the body. Understandably, this is a dilemma to any writer, because we absolutely have no existing language with the vocabulary to allow direct comparisons between the natural and the supernatural. And even if we did, we would lack the experience and subsequent knowledge to create a sufficient example, as those who may have advanced to the spirit world, should it exist, have not returned to help clarify the differences or present us with at least elementary analogies.

But one might consider this example: *water.* Under certain conditions water becomes ice or it becomes vapor. We clearly recognize these three physical states which it can assume and yet not be anything but water. That is, at anytime, it can be returned to its liquid state from its ice formation or from its vaporized form.

When it is ice, one may crack that ice, crush it, melt it, destroy it totally — but they are left with either a vapor or water. Is it probable that the connection between the soul, its body, and the eternal spiritual state is much the same as the connection between water, ice and vapor?

Now, of course, if when you walk away from this book you

visualize the soul as being a liquid which is solidified for life on earth and then vaporized for its spiritual existence in eternity, you have absolutely misinterpreted the example. It is simply the relationship hat is the point in the example, not the physical representation. Besides, in the example of the water and its states of exisence, we are dealing with simply a chemical substance with no mark of individuality let alone intelligence, but in the case of the soul we deal with a subject having a personal nature (or supernature) and intelligence.

Consider Aquinas' ideas on the three states of existence: the eternal, aeviternal and temporal. The three states are connected in some divine way but their spans into past and present vary. The soul belongs in aeviternity, the body in time. The soul, presumably, goes on forever, the body corrupts. But because it is not from eternity, it cannot be the same as God, though, of course it must be connected to God in some way to have life or to have been granted the privilege of existence in the first place — either through direct or indirect design. As aeviternity is a state between the temporal and eternal, it seems that the soul itself is the connection between the temporal and the spiritual.

Thus, to look upon the body is to look upon the soul. But to look for a connecting link between spiritual and physical phenomena is an unwarranted exercise, for the soul itself is the link and the body is the soul. It is sort of like looking for the link between ice and water. The water does not stop here and the ice begin there, the water is simply expressed as ice in a specific physical environment.

Does this imply that the soul has the same form as its body but it is invisible? No, it implies nothing of the sort. It is possible, however, that in the soul there exists the same types of perceptions, or the potential for the same types of perceptions and sensations as that of the body, but in its spiritual state the soul has the memory of them or the concept of them rather than the ability to actually experience them — as the blind man knows his roommate; as you remember laughter and a good time, and are aware of these, though in referencing the memory and understanding the effect of laughter and the feeling of a good time you are not actually experiencing them.

IV

There have been strictly materialistic interpretations of the soul-body (or, *mind-body*) problem in which all natural events, whether they be physical or mental, are explained in terms of scientific observations or laws. These theories tie together our sense-perceptions with our thoughts in a bi-directional perspective. For instance, in our formative years we are constantly monitoring sensations which we come to recognize, then store for memory, then recall at will. When we have them in memory they are no longer physical sensations, of course, but we remember them in terms of their physical results. Once in memory they are translated into thoughts. They are sensual experiences which have been converted to mental experiences. Once we have them as memories we can not only recall them at any given time but we may also use them as references to draw observations about other things which we may not yet come into contact with but which we are able to sense through any one or number of our senses.

A strictly materialistic interpretation, then, would have us accept that while indeed there is such a thing as a soul, and man *is* composed of body and soul, they are absolutely distinct and there is no connection between them. Any relation between what the body experiences and what the soul perceives as a result is simply by the intervention of some divine hand. The soul iself lacks the ability to associate any particular bodily sensation with any particular idea. The problem presented to this theory is that there *are* thoughts which originate somewhere that come into the brain seemingly *not* from experience: for instance, ontological ideas.

V

If one prefers to accept the premise that the soul is a strictly spiritual existence, then perhaps he must turn to Aquinas for the most sufficient explanation of the connection between soul and body — or to Aristotle on whom Aquinas based his own ideas. But Aquinas' ideas on the soul seem to flow in a deeper and more consistent logic and he seems to be the one philospher who was most ambitious and fearless (of challenge) in tackling the subject of the soul. Some of his ideas have already been covered in this book but are covered again below simply to make his thoughts on the spiritual connection so much more coherent.

To Aquinas, the soul is the first principle of life. It is definitely not a material form but, rather, the *act* of some material form just as heat, which is the principle by which things become hot, is not a body but an act of a body. The human soul, also referred to as the intellect or the mind, is both incorporeal and subsistent.

Aquinas stressed that the human body "is necessary for the action of the intellect not as its organ of action, but by reason of the object; for the phantasm is to the intellect what color is to sight." But this dependence of the soul upon the abilities of the body does not prove the intellect "to be non-subsistant; otherwise it would follow that an animal is non-subsistent since it requires external sensible things in order to sense."[8]

The *intellectual soul* has no form and is definitely not composed of matter. If it did consist of matter and form, "the forms of things would be received into it as individuals, and so it would only know the individual; just as it happens with the sensitive powers which receive forms in a corporeal organ, since matter is the principle of which forms are individualized." Any intellectual substance which has knowledge of nature absolutely, as in the way the soul knows a stone absolutely as a stone, must in itself be without composition of matter and form.

Aquinas claimed that when we consider the way in which the intellect operates (which he explains in his answer to question 76)[9] we must come to admit that the intellectual principle is united to the body as its form.

Aquinas referred to Aristotle's treatment of this subject: " . . . we can wholly dismiss as unnecessary the question whether the soul and the body are one: it is as meaningless as to ask whether the wax and the shape given to it by the stamp are one, or generally the matter of a thing and that of which it is the matter." Aristotle goes on in his explanation to describe the soul much as one would the formula which defines the essence of a thing. The soul, to Aristotle, is the essential character of the body to which it is assigned.[10]

Aquinas, in his own explanation of the spiritual connection, stressed that "just as the shape is united to the wax without a body intervening, therefore also the soul is united to the body."

Is the soul in each part of the body?

Aquinas answered that since the soul may be inferred to be in

85

each part of the body not in regard to each of the body's powers but in the sense, for example, that, regarding sight, it is in the eye; regarding hearing, it is in the ear, etc. "We must observe, however," he wrote, "that since the soul requires diversity of parts, its relation to the whole is not the same as its relation to the parts; for the whole it is compared primarily and essentially, as to its proper and proportionate perfectibility, but to the parts, secondarily, in so far as they are ordered to the whole."

One cannot accept Aristotle's example of the wax as one meant to be an exact analogy. It is simply symbolic in the sense that the drawing of the logic symbol for an AND gate or a flip-flop is for an electronic engineer, symbolic of the circuits which they are meant to represent. The actual circuits perform exactly as indicated by the binary codes represented at the input or output bits of the drawings, but the actual circuits do not look like the symbols and have various voltages at their input and output bits instead of binary values. There is absolutely no correlation between the configurement of the true circuits and the drawings which represent them but the functions of these circuits can be duly represented by means of the drawings and binary assignments for relative voltage levels.

Spiritual and physical bodies can have little in common except, perhaps, of course, in absolutely general terms, as in existence, knowledge, direction, etc. Thus the reason why any examples to show the spiritual connection between mind and body must always be destined to fall far short of success. Aristotle's example of the wax and its form is insufficient, for to destroy (not *change*) the physical form is to destroy the wax, so we understand completely the relationship between the wax and its form. But in the case of the soul and its physical form, when the body dies we are left with physical remains, so the soul must be connected to the body in such a way as to allow body and soul to become separated at death; perhaps in the way that a large body of water may turn with the tide away from that part of it formed as ice near the shore.

VI

If one prefers to consider things on a simply physical level, then perhaps she might want to combine the ideas of those teleologists, like Paley, who offer that it is within the range of possibility for the soul to be an incredibly minute form that contains the coding for generating individual forms. As Paley pointed out, when we consider that basic substances from which we originated, we find no relation. That is, there is nothing in the sperm and the egg to ever give hint that what will eventually develop will be something so complex and efficiently designed that it will be human.

And if we add to this basic concept the scientific theories of conservation of energy, whereupon we surmise that nothing in the universe is finally destroyed, we realize that there might be an elementary organic form that continues on without destruction. Thus, the soul in all its simplicity is capable of extension under given circumstances, and contraction during that event we call death — or shedding, if you will, of its more obvious physical form — but remains intact with all its formulae until it is once again in a position to grow physically.

In this purely teleological, or materialistic approach, the theories of Descartes, of Leibnitz, and of many others all have a place in the challenging picture puzzle of the soul.

CHAPTER 9
The Religious Arguments

In surveying some of the religious arguments for immortality, one might begin by considering those that rest upon teleological foundations. In Chapter 6 of this book, Kant's ideas were reviewed; in these he expressed that once one considers the wisdom and goodness of the deity he has good reason to presume that an opportunity for eternal existence will be made available to each and every person, if only so that each and every one will have the chance to reach that full potential for which they have begun to strive here in this life. This same idea threads throughout Christian philosophy. In Christianity, the purpose of life is seen as an opportunity to develop oneself toward worthiness of final union with God. In this life, however, there is no time to reach one's full potential and if there were it is certainly evident that God is not here on earth, so any union with him must take place in another world, another dimension, another way. If it is in the divine plan, as Christians recognize it to be, that men and women one day "see" God, then another existence beyond this one is absolutely necessary.

Christianity has never interpreted that the moral life should be lived for is own sake. At its very fundamental level, Christianity is highly subjective. Each man and woman who welcomes the Catholic or Protestant doctrines does so with the ultimate aim of qualifying for eternal life with God. That such individually selfish aims should result in a higher quality of life for all is due to the nature of God, who, as the personification of the *highest good,* represents and wishes all motives and behavior which not only finally benefit the individual but the entire Christian community. But this emphasis of Christianity on personal salvation as the final objective of faith stresses what ultimately is the worth of the individual before God. God loves the individual as much as he loves the community. He cares for the individual as much as he cares for the community. The Christian God is a personal God. He wishes the ultimate happiness of each man and woman. That happiness in its most august form is not possible here on earth; and if at times it may be, it can never be consistent, given the nature of the material world in which we live. Another world must be designed for that, another life.

When Teilhard de Chardin was searching for a reason to justify moral life, to justify a moral philosophy, he wrote that he began to realize "that the discovery in and around me of a nascent spirit meant nothing at all if that spirit were not immortal."[1] He explained that *to him* he words immortality and irreversibility are synonymous and that in his view of the order of things, the universe can never be stopped from continuing its evolution toward new levels of freedom and consciousness. This same idea holds for *spirit.* It, too, is constantly growing in knowledge, in consciousness. Individual perfection, of course, has not yet evolved but the "collective powers of spirit have increased to an impressive degree."[2] One might interpret Teilhard's meaning to be that if the general direction of spirit is indeed irreversible, then in witnessing its growth one witnessess its part in eternity. Teilhard, by the way, went on to write that he felt it was unfathomable for him to consider any spiritual evoluton which did not find its omega "in a supreme personality." But he qualifies this statement later on. First, however, he points out that to him it would be of little concern if, once the sum of his life has evolved into immortal existence, his personality were to be fused with a being who was greater in all respects than he. However, as willing as he was to accept such total destruction of his individuality, the truth is that in becoming a part of God (of the Great Whole, as he puts it), one's individuality *is not* lost. Rather, when man's incorporation with God finally takes place, he will find himself "personally immortalized . . . For the human monad, fusion with the universe means super-personalization."[3]

Teilhard's ideas have not been fully evaluated in terms of how they blend or excite the traditional Christian doctrine, but his emphasis, nonetheless, is still personal immortalization, although the terms on which he puts it are beyond what is usually understood as personal immortality, beyond what is the usually figurative interpretation of the afterlife. But to Christian leaders of all times, the higher levels of religious awareness have always been underplayed for they have generally been deemed unsuited for the congregations of relatively uneducated or unsophisticated thinkers. Theologians know that any type of attempt to explain a future spiritual existence is simply an exercise in speculation and one that will not be easily comprehended by the community. Traditionally, people are more inclined to accept the idea of an afterlife when it is described in purely materialistic terms, as in the case of heaven or hell. Heaven and hell exist up there somewhere or down there somewhere where as habitats for strictly spiritual forms heaven and hell can have no relative location to the physical universe. And the inhabitants of heaven are identified by halos, possibly wings also; Heaven has turf and vegetation; God wears a beard. It's all mere artistry and religious nonsense. Jesus of Nazareth never attempted to paint such pictures in the minds of his followers. Rather, when he talked of the kingdom of God he did it metaphorically: Heaven was always "as" or "like" something with which his audience could identify; but it was never described specifically or given a location. Jesus understood how impractical it would be to impress upon his loyal but unsophisticated followers that a spiritual kingdom could not be concerned with material things.

That "monad" of which Teilhard spoke has always been interpreted by the Christian sects to be a spiritual one. Thus, science can never threaten the philosophy of the soul and of immortality, for science is ultimately concerned with natural things, religion ultimately with the supernatural. Christians see each other as essentially spiritual beings in temporary physical form. Thus, the corruption of the physical casing within which the spirit operates in no way threatens the existence of the individual soul.

In Christianity, immortality has always meant personal immortality, and a type of personal immortality well beyond what Teilhard sensed. To consider an afterlife which means total negation of individuality is to stand against a fundamental belief of Christianity. This idea of personal immortality is necessary to Protestant and Catholic thinkers because of the way they interpret inherent nature (or, rather, *spirit*) and in the way they interpret biblical passages. In short, it is highly unlikely that God, in all his majesty and wisdom, would work in vain — that is, be satisfied with less than what can be, be content with beings who on final analysis are incomplete, be content with temporal rather than eternal things. And, as the *highest good,* he is unlikely to offer less than he might. And of the two possibilities that follow, which would you consider to be the higher good: (1) a life given to the complete development of its consciousness only to be ultimately destroyed; or, (2) a life so described but now given the privilege of continuance?

But, of course, in Christianity, while immortality is guaranteed, happiness, or just the freedom from pain, is not. Some might very well make it to that place or state where God exists; others might never make it at all; and still others may be directed to detour to some other place for temporal punishment. There are always the fires of hell or purgatory for sinners just as sure as there is a heaven for the blessed. Rarely does it dawn on those who take religion at a purely ceremonial level that an immaterial life, such as a soul, is hardly likely to be effected by actual fire; but, nevertheless, even the very devout fear an eternity in the flames of hell. Today, Christian theologians, if they care to even consider the possibility of eternal punishment beyond the deprivation of the "vision" of God, use the term "fire" symbolically, leaving it up to each individual to ponder whether that final punishment is simply lack of privilege or actual punishment that would be to the spirit what fire is to the body.

II

In Buddhism, the question of an afterlife is never directly considered. When Gautama Siddhartra (Buddha) outlined his beliefs for the faithful, he admitted that there were some questions which were beyond man's ability to answer, and would therefore only result in keeping each man and woman from pursuing other questions, the answers of which *would* add to their own spiritual development. There is a state in the Buddhist religion called Nirvana which one eventually reaches when he has overcome all temptation. Exactly where Nirvana is, or what it consists, Buddha never explained.

In the older form of the religion known as Hinayan Buddhism, the soul was not seen as a separate entity. In short, the Hinayan Buddhist saw no possibility of a personal immortality and, in fact, saw no God who watched over and judged humanity. This early form of the religion was definitely atheistic, yet it held that rebirth was possible and that in whatever way salvation occurred, it occurred due to the individual's ability to live his life in such a way that he eliminated all misery.

In Mayhana Buddhism, the idea is introduced of a savior who allows individuals to go through countless rebirths for their eventually salvation. But this savior is not "God;" the savior to Buddhists refers more to an office which at one time or another each man will be privileged to hold during his evolution toward Nirvana.

In Japanese Mayhana Buddhism, there has always been a strong emphasis on the future life. In this variation of the religion, the soul of each man and woman travels an incredible journey from this life to its final destiny. But whether or not the soul arrives at this final destination as an individual entity depends probably upon one's personal beliefs. And whether or not there is a "God" at this final destination is never clearly stated in the Japanese sect.

III

The emphasis in Confucianism has always been on the harmony in human relationships. Confucians have traditioanlly been little concerned with the prospect of an afterlife. What may become of an individual after his or her life on earth seems always to have been a topic widely avoided. Moral principle is the motto of Confucianism and the religion has always represented a movement far more concerned with physical rather than spiritual life.

IV

Whether or not Hinduism can be defined as a religion is often debated. It is not so much a way of worship founded on faith as it is a way of life which has evolved from centuries of experience. But Hinduism accepts the reality of a Supreme Being and like Christianity defines God as a trinity of beings. There is Brahma who is the sole creator of the universe, Veshner who takes the role of preserver, and Shiva who plays the part of destroyer. Again, as in Christianity, Hinduism stresses the spiritual over the mere physical. A man and a woman may, in fact, experience many lives. This is an idea defined as "the transmigration of souls." Those who live a moral existence will return again in a more pure physical state until one day they have achieved such favor in the eyes of God that they need no longer return to physical life. On the other hand, if they have lived an immoral existence, then they are doomed to return to life in lesser bodies, even animal bodies, until they effectively work their way back up the scale and into favor with God. While the Hindus do indeed acknowledge the existence of God and the individual soul, the religion does not define what God's final plan is or what may be the final destiny of the soul. There is, however, a reference to an eternal abode, but this comes to men and women only by the grace of God.

V

In the Islamic religion, there is also a greater emphasis on the spiritual than on the physical. And, as in the Christian religion, there are the fires of Hell for those who turn away from the true God, and the joys of an eternal paradise for those who submit to the will of the true God. The final destiny of the soul is its union with the one true God.

VI

In Judaism, the stress has always been on righteousness. Righteousness is the key to salvation. God will reward or punish in the life to come as men and women so deserve. Yet, though Judaism is the source religion from which both the Christian and Islamic religions grew, the Jews, in practice, have put little emphasis on the world to come. This may very well be because in the Jewish religion, God is seen as being just as concerned with establishing a kingdom here on earth as he is in maintaining his spiritual kingdom.

VII

Atheism is not a religion, but it will be discussed briefly nonetheless.

In atheism, the idea of immortality, strangely enough, is an idea which does not meet with total rejection. For the most part, atheists are pessimists in a philosophical sense and see life as accidental and without true meaning. But there have been noted atheists, among them J.E. McTaggart, who saw the possibility of continued existence beyond this life.

The type of immortality of which an atheist generally admits, however, is not a personal immortality. It represents, more or less, a type of atomic fusion. It is, for the most part, based on the law of conservation of energy, which states that the energy of the universe is never lost (see chapter on the teleological argument) and, therefore, probably the fundamental physical element of the individual is not entirely lost either but, instead, goes on to live again in some form, or as a part of some form.

———————

CHAPTER 10
Summary

Eternal and immortal are two terms which many dictionaries define in the same way but their meanings are entirely different in philosophy and theology. Immortal implies that while something was indeed at one time brought into existence it can never finally be eliminated but will, instead, continue to exist in some form forever. Eternal implies the same guarantee of foreverness but that which eternal is said to never have had a beginning.

ETERNITY

Eternity is generally described in terms of either an infinite duration in either direction — into the past as well as into the future —or in terms of complete timelessness. The very concept of eternity is indeed a tough one to grasp! The thought of someone or something having always been in existence is, at first, seemingly absurd. But against the only other possibility — that something or someone one day suddenly appeared from nothing — the idea of eternity comes to be much more plausible.

Aquinas has explained for us in his *Summa Theologica* that in every movement there is a series of successions which have occurred before or after the others. This series of successions enables us to understand this intellectually elusive thing called time. Time, he emphasized, is the measure of what occurs before and after in every movement. If there is no movement there is no before and after. If there is no before and after there can be no time. "As, therefore, the nature of time consists in the numbering of before and after in movement, so likewise is the understanding of the uniformity of *whatever* is completely outside of movement consists the nature of eternity." He adds to his argument that whatever is immoveable cannot.have succession and, therefore, no beginning and no end. "Thus, we have two reasons for believing in eternity," he concludes. "The first is that what is eternal is interminable — which is to say, it has no beginning and no end, for it has no term in either way; the second is that eternity lacks succession because eternity is simultaneously whole."

Aquinas borrowed some of his ideas from a 6th century Roman philosopher named Boethius (480-524) who saw eternity as the total possession of infinite life all at once. To Boethius, the only things that can possibly possess eternal life are those which can contain wholly and simultaneously the entire fullness of unending life, which at one time possesses the future with the past, and this thing in existence must be ever capable of controlling and aiding itself as well as to keep present within itself changing time in its infinity.

But Boethius' distinguishing of time from eternity was, again, no original idea. Before him Plotinus (205-270) put forth similar arguments. Plotinus saw time as no more than a mimic of eternity. He wrote that whatever it is that time absorbs and seals to itself of what remains permanent in eternity will eventually be destroyed in its temporal state, saved otherwise only because in some degree it still belongs to eternity. However, he pointed out, whatever exists in time stands to be totally destroyed if it is unreservedly absorbed in time.

In his *Third Ennead,* he again emphasizes that eternity and time are two completely different things, eternity having its existence in what he calls the *everlasting kind* and time having its existence only through possession and only in the universe that we understand. In the *Third Ennead,* he wrote that eternity requires something essentially complete though it is without sequence. " . . . It cannot be satisfied by something measured out to some more remote time or even by something limitless, but, in its limitless reach, still having the progression of futurity. It requires something which is immediately possessed of the fullness of being, something whose being is not at all dependent upon any quantity but rather subsists before all quantity."

After Aquinas, there were many other philosophers who became, during sometime in their careers, preoccupied with the subject of eternity. Among them:

- Michel De Montaigne (1533-1592), who wrote that time is no measure of eternity, for eternity both precedes and follows time. That which is eternal is immutable and never had a beginning nor ever shall have an end.

- John Locke (1632-1704), who described eternity in terms of it encircling time, and God, at His eternal throne, has control of the past, present and future *all at once.* As Locke saw it, what lies in the future lies there until it finally occurs; man cannot reach out to it and make it present for any length of time. And what lies in the past for man lies there forever, never to be retrieved by man. But with God, it is possible to recall the past and make present the future.

Some philosophers have argued that there is an eternal cosmic life cycle, often referred to as cyclical recurrence, which assures that universal events will occur over and over again. Plotinus liked this idea and in his *Fifth Ennead* he wrote that there may very well be identical reproduction of someone from one cosmic period to another. He stressed, however, that there cannot be such identical reproduction during the same period.

Augustine confronted this unusual idea of cyclical recurrence and in his *City of God* he argued against rather than for it. And most Christian philosophers have followed Augustine's stand. For one thing, the idea goes too strongly against the concept of each man's individuality as well as his relationship with God, which, in Christianity, is based on a final union with Christ and complete adherence to the will of God, all culminating in a last judgement. Besides, according to Aquinas, even God does not possess the power to recreate identical individuals because that in itself is a contradiction, and God is not of a contradictory nature.

After Aquinas, the general attitude toward cyclical recurrence continued to be somewhat negative. Frederick Nietzche (1844-1900), however, saw a great deal of merit in it and believed there was unquestionnable scientific truth to the concept. He could envision himself coming back time and time again, and, therefore, would be, as every man should be, compelled to make his life one which was worth returning to. Charles Sanders Pierce (1839-1914) also argued for the scientific basis and probability of cyclical recurrence.

Now the idea of eternity and the idea of God are so closely related that it is impossible to think of the one without the other.

There are, of course, no conclusive philosophical proofs for either the existence of God or the existence of such a state as eternity but there are, of course, very weighty arguments which stand stronger than the arguments that would disprove either of these ideas as reality. The primary philosophical arguments for the existence of God are the ontological, cosmological, teleological and moral arguments. there are secondary arguments, also: those from common consent, degrees of perfection and religious experience.

One of the necessary attributes of God is eternalness. If there is no such thing as eternity, then there cannot be such a thing as God, for He must be limitless, and limitlessness implies eternalness.

Aristotle (384-322 BC) saw God as the prime mover of the heavens and the earth and believed that, as such, He exists out of necessity. As a necessary being He must also exist for the good.

Aristotle saw all of life belonging to God, "for the actuality of thought is life, and God is that actuality; and God's self-dependent actuality is life most good and *eternal*. We say, therefore, that God is a living being, *eternal*, most good, so that life and duration continuous and eternal belong to God; for this is God."

Plotinus argued that eternity is the order of the supremely great and that on investigation it proved to be identical with God. " . . . it may fitly be described," he wrote, "as God made manifest, as God declaring what He is, as existence without jolt or change, and therefore as also the firmly living."

Aquinas wrote in his *Summa Theologica* that the idea of eternity follows logically from the concept of immutability just as the idea of time follows logically from the concept of movement. "As God is argued to be absolutely immutable, it follows, then, that God is eternal." Eternity, according to Aquinas, is none other than God Himself.

Immanuel Kant's ideas were similar. He saw God as "*one,* simple, all-efficient, and eternal."

Now, in addition to the concepts of eternity and time, there is also the concept of another state or dimension which exists between the two. It is called aeviternity. It is distinguished from eternity and time according to the following definitions:

> **eternity** — a state which has had *no beginning* and will have *no end.*
>
> **aeviternity** — a state which has had *a beginning* but will have *no end.*
>
> **time** — a state that has both *a beginning* and *an end.*

Aquinas adds that time has newness and oldness but aeviternity has no newsness and oldness.

Aeviternity, then, would be that state in which the human soul resides. It is the guarantee of immortality for that which is assigned to it.

To this point, then, we see that there have been thousands of years of arguments which point to the probabilty of an eternal state. Something must be of an eternal nature. There must be something which has had no beginning. There is nothing we know of that has come from nothing at all.

But that which has always been in existence, many argue, may not necessarily be that which we refer to as God. It could very well be a gas, a force of energy of any kind. It need not be an individual and a person as we have come to conceive God.

But there are overwhelming arguments for the existence of God and the necessity of visualizing Him as the prime mover, the designer of life, the moral commander . . . and having, especially, the attribute of perfection. Not to possess eternalness would contradict the idea of perfection, so God must exist eternally.

Knowing at least that there is state which can have no beginning or end and there is at least a state (aeviternity) in which things can come into existence and remain in existence, we have, then, the hope of immortality, though not the guarantee.

IMMORTALITY

As far back as the 7th century B.C. there was a Greek poet-philosopher who wrote that the soul of every man and woman had an afterlife. His name was Orpheus and the writings and stories attributed to him influenced another great philosopher named Pythogoras who developed further the idea that the psyche — or soul — was not mortal at all but rather a part of some universal force from which it had become separated and eventually imprisoned in the mortal bodies of men and women. One day, according to Pythogoras, the souls of men and women would return to their eternal parent.

The ideas of Pythogoras, in turn, had noticeable influence on Socrates and then Plato, who adopted, among others, Pythogoras' arguments for the immortality of the soul. Their ideas, of course, were carried forward to the time of Plotinus. Plotinus himself believed that life is inherent in the soul. He wrote that . . . "given soul, all material things become collaborators with the life principle to bring about an orderly cosmos; but without soul in the things of the universe, these things could not even exist let alone perform their functions. They only exist given soul; but soul can exist without them."

Aquinas agreed, though, of course, not with all the interpretations of the sometimes far-out Plotinus. Aquinas argued that the soul is an intellectual principle and it is incorruptible. It is a subsistant form and can never cease to exist.

Other philosophers have also argued for the existence and immortality of the soul. Among them:

- Philo Judaeus (20 BC - 40 AD), the Jewish Hellenistic philosopher, who argued that there are two types of souls, the rational and the irrational. Irrational souls come into being when the bodies of men and women are created; rational souls come into being at the time of creation. Only the rational souls can realize immortality and, then, only by the will of God.

- Avicenna (980-1037), the Islamic philosopher whose ideas Aquinas was well-familiar with, argued that the soul comes into existence when the body is created. But the soul possesses immortality whereas the body does not. When the body corrupts, the soul continues as a distinct individual.

- Marsilio Ficino (1433-1499), the Italian philosopher, brought together the arguments of Plato, Plotinus, Augustine, Averroes and Aquinas to make his argument for the necessity of immortality. Ficino saw the role of life as we know it as a means of finally reaching God. If physical life means the end of the individual, then there can be no final and eternal union with God. Therefore, the soul must be immortal.

- Thomas De Vio (1468-1534), also known as Cardinal Cajetan, saw any attempt to prove the immortality of the soul to be useless. There is no proof, or way of proving. The idea has to be accepted on faith alone. But he considered Avicenna's arguments to have some merits. Avicenna (9880-1037) believed the soul to be immaterial, and being so, it could not corrupt, could not die.

- Juan Luis Vives (1492-1540) saw the soul as the driving power in man but he also believed it was useless to search for the spiritual connection.

- Giordanno Bruno (1548-1600) defined the soul as a monad, and one very similar to those which make up the basic elements of the universe.

- John Locke (1632-1716) believed that the soul possessed intelligence despite the fact that it was an immaterial existence. But it needs bodily form in order to apply that intelligence to learning experiences. He, too, believed that the soul was the driving force in living things.

- Spinoza, in his *Ethics,* demonstrated that the human mind must possess an eternal quality which allows it to exist after the body has died.

- Immanual Kant (1724-1804), the German philosopher, wrote that for an individual to realize the *summum bonum* it was necessary for him to have an afterlife, for there is no possible way of attaining the highest good in this life.

- Andrew Seth Pringle-Pattison (1856-1931), the Scottish philosopher, believed that immortality was possible but not guaranteed. He was unable to believe that a good and perfect God would destroy that which He has created — or let it be destroyed. However, he could very well envision some selectivity on the part of God concerning who should or should not be entitled to an afterlife.

- The Islamic metaphysician, Muhammed Iqbal (1877-1938), believed that the soul was created to be free and as it nears a perfection closer to that of God, it becomes ever more free. It approaches God in terms of perfection but not in terms of submergence.

There is, of course, no conclusive proof that there is life beyond this one. And, perhaps, those who argue for its existence may be, as Ludwig Feuerbach (1804-1872) commented, influenced solely by their own egos which are in natural revolt to the thought of their own final death.

Is there any scientific proof of an afterlife?

There is, at least, those well-founded theories of an unchanging quantity of universal energy and the incorruptible nature of basic elements. And there are the teleological arguments.

By teleology is meant the search for goal-directed activity in the natural world.

Thus, there is a special attraction to any teleological argument. Teleological arguments concern themselves with natural things that we can sense in one way or another. They may be abstract — as in the case of intellectual ability, creative ability, goodness — and we cannot see or touch them but we can realize them by their results.

And we all know that as we grow older and our physical characteristics fall into disrepair, those qualities which are intellectual and those instincts based on intellectual observations, grow stronger. Observing this same phenomena, Immanuel Kant wrote: "In the wisdom of the Supreme Being, and in the shortness of life, so inadequate to the development of the glorious powers of human nature, we may ... find sufficient grounds for a doctrinal belief in the future life of the human soul."

But if this Supreme Being does exist, in his infinite power could He not have created pure souls in a state of eternal happiness? Why the need for a temporary state in the immortal or eternal life of the soul? Is there a purpose for this transitional period in the life of the soul? Many great philosophers, as well as great men and women from all walks of life, see existence as essentially meaningless; that is, they felt, or feel, that life on this earth has no future meaning; someday all will end and because everything is temporary, everything is, in the final analysis, worthless.

Some writers and philosophers, like Bertrand Russell and Arthur Schopenhauer, are typical of the negative attitude toward life and its meaning. Russell saw little proof of immortality and Schopenhauer claimed that for him life was so meaningless that if he were given the choice of accepting or rejecting it, he would choose the latter alternative.

Pessimism has its points. There is war, sickness, physical defects, hate . . . But in all cases, injustice, social and economic misery are not the designs of God but rather accidents of the interplay between men and women.

In the case of what appear to be injustices in the natural world (sickness, etc.), one cannot deny that evil exists, but it is never "natural" in the following sense. There is a way in which the universe is designed to work. Through ignorance, eagerness, selfishness, carelessness, men and women interfere with that design, and in so doing put themselves in harms way. And in all cases where the irresponsibility of men and women to each other prevails, what harm does follow is of their own doing, is certainly never the design of God.

William Paley reminded us in his *Natural Theology* that when God created the human species there was one of three attitudes He might have assumed:

1. He wished the happiness of all;
2. He wished the misery of all;
3. He was completely indifferent to each and everyone's happiness or misery.

But if he wished misery upon men and women He would certainly have made our senses instruments of pain rather than instruments of gratification and enjoyment. "He mighst have made, for example, everything we tasted bitter; everything we saw loathsome; everything we touched a sting; every smell a stench; and every sound a discord."

Paley explained that there is no doubt that evil exists, but it is never, that we can perceive, the object of any willfull design. Teeth ache but that is not what they are designed to do; they are designed, rather, to facilitate eating. If any anatomist comes upon a part of the body which he cannot comprehend, he does not look to find the pain which it causes the body but for the benefit which he assumes it must be designed.

Aquinas had written long before Paley that evil has no formal cause; it is, more than anything, "a privation of form; neither has it a final cause, but rather is it a privation of order and to the proer end." Evil, according to Aquinas, happens by accident. There can be no effective argument that God is ever the cause of evil, for evil is caused by the defect of an action, by the defect of the agent; and in God there is no defect.

Many philosophers and theologians believed, or believe, that the purpose of life is to graduate us toward a complete union with God. Some have considered this to mean we will one day be completely reabsorbed into the mind of God. But Rudolph Christoph Euckin and Teilhard De Chardin give a somewhat different interpretation to this idea.

Life to Euckin is designed to lead the soul to ultimate truth. The soul is destined to become bound with God but not to such an extent that it will lose its individuality. It will, rather, become bound with God in terms of its perspective, its dedication to truth and intellectual beauty. Teilhard wrote that the purpose of life is to bring man ever closer to divine perfection; but it is within the realm of probability that God's intent is to share all of eternity with beings exactly like Himself.

But why must there be death? A life of trial? Why not bring forth unending life, perfect existences, all at once? Life, with its accidental trials builds individuality, individual responsibility. If God does indeed seek the companionship of men and women for eternity, He would receive little satisfaction in that friendship if these individual souls went to Him by command. Considering that in all things God, as we care to perceive Him, is interested in the highest good, then he would see the creation of individuals to be higher than that or mere robots, and a friendship created through willingness a higher good than one created by fear and command.

But what of this soul that will one day return to, or join, God in eternity? Where is it located wihin within the human condition?

Many philosophers have considered the question but the prospect of finding a physical office for something which may be completely spiritual is, by definition, completely impossible.

But the temptation to seek a material explanation for that which is assumed to be spiritual continues, and not necessarily to identify as much as to disapprove. Modern medical specialists probe the brain to discover its secrets, hoping to uncover at the same time the combination of electrical and chemical interactions which give it its driving force and its individuality.

If one does prefer to take a strictly materialistic perspective, then perhaps one might want to look at Paley's alternate explanation about the soul in which he sees it as the smallest possible element that exists, yet it contains the necessary "program" to develop into forms with characteristics completely different from those which it necessarily contains, as an egg, having no physical relation to the chick which will be born from it, contains the necessary elements to bring into existence a winged animal. The egg has no wings and if you crack it open once it is produced, you will not find inside of it some physical puzzle of legs, eyes, etc. that time will put together as the hen heats it with her body. Consider now in human biology the male sperm fertilizing the female's egg and we see nothing in either the sperm or the egg at their first meeting that would indicate arms, legs, head, etc. in minute form, ready for growth yet what will eventually be produced will look nothing like the sperm or like the egg. Add to this observation the concept of energy conservation, wherein nothing in the universe is ever lost, and one adds argument for the immortality of this tiny element which contains as part of itself the electrical, chemical and physical potential of developing into a human individual.

If one prefers to see the soul as a strictly spiritual existence, there is for study Aquinas' ideas. To him, the soul is the first principle of life. It is not a material existence but the act of some material form. An example would be *heat,* which is the principle by which things become hot, is not a body but an act of a body.

Aquinas saw the connection between body and soul in much the same way as did Aristotle. As a matter of fact, he repeated one of Aristotle's examples to drive home his own argument. Aquinas asks us to consider wax. Its shape is united to the wax without any connecting body — in the same way the body is connected to the soul.

The religious attitudes on immortality by Christians, Buddhists, Confucians, Hindus, Muslims, Jews, and atheists differ markedly.

The Christians believe that this life is a training ground whereby members of the Christian community and others who live for the highest good will earn the privilege of final union with God. The Christian God is a personal God who desires the ultimate happiness of each man and woman. But such happiness is not possible here on Earth; therefore there must be another life where it can be realized.

In Buddhism, the idea of an afterlife is little more than that — that is, little more than idea. But there are many forms of Buddhism. In Hinayan Buddhism, fundamentally atheistic, there is no God, no hope of immortality. In Mayhana Buddhism, there are many lives to be lived as one approaches an eternal future in Nirvana. In Japanese Mayhana Buddhism, the emphasis has always been on immortality, but whether or not it is a personal or impersonal immortality is not clear.

Confucians have always emphasized the here and now and the search for harmony in all relationships. The idea of immortality is not a specific concern in Confucianism.

Hinduism is not a religion for it does not bind fast its members to a way of worship as does Christianity, Judaism, Buddhism and other religions. But the Hindus stress the spiritual over the physical and the idea of the transmigration of souls. But what may be God's final plan for the soul of every man or woman is never directly addressed.

The Muslims also stress the spiritual over the physical. In the Islamic religion, the final state for the human soul is union with God.

Judaism has never actually tackled the question of immortality because it has always evolved from the concept of a transcendental deity that is well beyond man's understanding. Thus, the plans of this deity are also beyond man's comprehension. The search for the fact or falsehood of immortality, then, is a futile one, for the answer lies with God whom we cannot understand.

Atheism is not a religion but it does consider the possibility of an impersonal immortality based on the idea of atomic fusion and the law of conservation of energy. The fundamental physical properties of an individual will never be entirely lost though this property may go on to exist as part of another form.

NOTES

CHAPTER 1

1. Saint Thomas Aquinas. "Summa Theologica," Part 1, Quest. 2, Art. 3 in *Thomas Aquinas,* Vol. 1. Translated by Fathers of the Dominican English Province. ed. Robert Maynard Hutchins (Chicago: Encyclopedia Britannica Great Books of the Western World 1952), p. 13.

2. *Ibid.*

3. *Ibid.*

4. *Ibid.,* Quest. 10, Articles 1 & 4, pp. 41 & 43.

5. Aristotle. "Physics," in *Aristotle.* Trans. R.P. Hardie and R.K. Gaye. ed. Robert Maynard Hutchines (Chicago: Encyclopedia Britannica Great Books of the Western World, 1952), p. 300.

6. Aristotle. "Metaphysics," Bk. 14, Ch. 2, in *Aristotle.* Trans. W.D. Ross, ed. Robert Maynard Hutchins (Chicago: Encyclopedia Britannica Great Books of the Western World, 1952) pp. 620-621.

7. Plato. "Timaeus," in *Plato.* Trans. Benjamin Jawett, ed. Robert Maynard Hutchins (Chicago: Encyclopedia Britannica Great Books of the Western World, 1952), pp. 447-456.

8. *Ibid.,* p. 450.

9. Michel Eyquem Montaigne, "Essais," Book 2, Ch. 12 in *Montaigne.* Trans. Charles Colton, ed. W. Carew Hazlitt (Chicago: Encyclopedia Britannica Great Books of the Western World, 1952), p. 293.

10. Saint Augustine. "City of God," Book 12, Ch. 13 in *Augustine.* Trans. Marcus Dods, ed. Robert Maynard Hutchins (Chicago: Encyclopedia Britannica Great Books of the Western World, 1952), p. 350.

11. Friedrich Nietzche. *The Will to Power.* Trans. W. Kaufman and R.J. Hollingdale (New York: Random House, 1967), p. 35.

CHAPTER 2

1. William Paley. "Natural Theology," Ch. 3 in *The Works of William Paley* (Edinburgh: Brown & Nelson, 1825) p. 526.

2. *Ibid.*

3. A summary of Anselm's ideas from Chapters 2-4 in his *Proslogion.*

4. Aquinas, "Summa Theologica," Question 2, Reply 2, p. 11.

5. Immanuel Kant, "Critique of Pure Reason," 2nd Div., Bk. 2, Ch. 3, Sect. 5 from *Kant,* trans. J.M.D. Meiklejohn, ed. Robert Maynard Hutchins (Chicago: Encyclopedia Britannica Great Books of the Western World, 1952), p. 182.

6. Aquinas, Question 2, Article 3, p. 13.

7. Aristotle, "Physics," Book 8, Chapter 6, pp. 344-346.

8. *Ibid.*

9. Aristotle. "Metaphysics," Book 8, Ch. 6 in *Aristotle.* Trans. W.D. Ross, ed. Robert Maynard Hutchins (Chicago: Encyclopedia Britannica Great Books of the Western World, 1952) pp. 345.

10. *Ibid.*

11. Aquinas, Question 10, Article 2, p. 42.

12. Kant, p. 176.

13. Aquinas, Question 10, Articles 2 & 3, pp. 41-43.

CHAPTER 3

1. Paley, Ch. 24, p. 531.

2. *Ibid.*

3. Aquinas, Question 10, Article 5, p. 44.

4. Augustine, "City of God," Bk. 12, Ch. 16, p. 352.

5. *Ibid.*

6. Paley, Ch. 27, p. 553.

CHAPTER 4

1. Plato, "Phaedrus," in *Plato*. Trans. Benjamin Jawett, ed. Robert Maynard Hutchins (Chicago: Encyclopedia Britannica Great Books of the Western World, 1952) p. 124.

2. *Ibid.*

3. Plotinus, "The Six Enneads," the 4th Ennead, 7th Tractate, 3rd Chapter, in *Plotinus*. Trans. Stephen McKenna, ed. Robert Maynard Hutchins (Chicago: Encyclopedia Britannica Great Books of the Western World, 1952, p. 192.

4. Aquinas, Quest. 75, Art. 5, p. 382.

5. *Ibid.*

CHAPTER 6

1. Kant, *"Critique of Pure Reason,"* Ch. 2, Sect. 3 of Transcendental Doctrine, in *Kant,* p. 242.

CHAPTER 7

1. Paley, Ch. 26, p. 536 1836.

2. Aquinas, "Summa Theologica," Part 1 of the Second Part, Quest. 1, Article 1, p. 609.

3. *Ibid.*, First Part, Quest. 49, Article 1, p. 265.

CHAPTER 8

1. Isaac Asimov, *The Human Brain, Its Capacities and Functions* (New York: New American Library, 1965) p. 85.

2. *Ibid.*

3. Aquinas, "Summa Theologica," Quest. 75, Article 1, pp. 378-379.

4. *Ibid,* p. 397.

5. *Ibid,* Article 2, p. 379.

6. *Ibid,* p. 380.

7. *Ibid.*

8. *Ibid., Question 76, Article 1, p. 386.*

9. *Ibid.*

10. *Ibid., Quest. 76, Article 1.*

11. *Ibid., Quest. 76, Article 1.*

CHAPTER 9

1. Pierre Teilhard De Chardin, *Christianity and Evaluation* (New York: Harcourt Bruce Javonovich, 1969) p. 109.

2. *Ibid., 109.*

3. *Ibid.,* 117.

WORKS CONSULTED

(Asterisk designates sources for translations
and other works from which excerpts were taken.)

*Aristotle. "Metaphysics," in *Aristotle,* trans. W.D. Ross, ed. Robert Maynard Hutchins. Chicago: Encyclopedia Britannica Great Books of the Western World, 1952. 499-631.

* — "Physics," in *Arisotle,* trans. R.P. Hardie and R.K. Gaye, ed. Robert Maynard Hutchins. Chicago: Encyclopedia Great Books of the Western World, 1952. 259-355.

*Augustine, Saint. "City of God," in *Augustine,* trans. Marcus Dods, ed. Robert Maynard Hutchins. Chicago: Encyclopedia Britannica Great Books of the Western World, 1952.

* — "Confessions," in *Augustine,* trans. Marcus Dods, ed. Robert Maynard Hutchins. Chicago: Encyclopedia Britannica Great Books of the Western World, 1952.

Asimov , Isaac. *The Human Brain, Its Capacities and Functions.* New York: New American Library, 1965.

*Boethius, Anicius. *De Consolatione Philosophiae,* trans. W.V. Cooper. New York: Carlton House. 30-120.

Cassirer, Ernst. *Kant's Life and Thought,* trans. James Haden. New Haven: Yale U. Press, 1981.

Dar, B.A. "Muhammed Iqbal," *Encyclopedia of Philosophy.* New York: Macmillan, 1967, Vol. 4, 213.

DeWitt, Norman Wentworth. *Epicurus & His Philosophy.* Minneapolis: Univ. of Minn., 1964.

Durant, Will. *The Story of Philosophy, the Lives and Opinions of the Great Philosophers.* New York: Pocket Books, 1961.

Edwards, Paul. "Atheism," in *Encyclopedia of Philosophy.* New York: Macmillan, 1967. Vol. 1, 174-188.

Frost, S.E., Jr. *Basic Teachings of the Great Philosophers: A Survey of Their Basic Ideas.* New York: Doubleday, 1962.

Gardener, Patrick. "Arthur Schopenhauer," *Encyclopedia of Philosophy.* New York: Macmillan, 1967. Vol. 7, 325.

Guthrie, W.K.C., *A History of Greek Philosophy,* Vol. 1. Cambridge Univ. Press, 1971.

Horvath, Nicholas A. *Philosophy.* Woodbury, N.Y.: Barron's Educational Series, 1974.

*James, William. "The Principles of Psychology" in *William James,* ed. Robert Maynard Hutchins. Chicago: Encyclopedia Britannica Great Books of the Western World, 1952.

*Kant, Immanuel. "Critique of Pure Reason," in *Kant,* trans. J.M.D. Meiklejohn, ed. Robert Maynard Hutchins. Chicago: Encyclopedia Great Books of the Western World, 1952.

Kenny, Anthony. *Aquinas,* ed. Keith Thomas. New York: Hill & Wang, 1980.

Mackenzie, J.S. "Eternity," in *Encyclopedia of Religion and Ethics,* Vol. 5, New York: Charles Scribner, 1967.

Mallone, S.H. "Immortality," in *Encyclopedia of Religion and Ethics,* Vol. 7, New York: Charles Scribner, 1967.

Muirden, James. *The Amateur Astronomer's Handbook: A Guide to Exploring the Heavens.* New York: Harper & Row, 3rd Edition, 1983.

Nietzche, Friedrich. The Will to Power, trans. W. Kaufman and R.J. Hollingdale. New York: Random House, 1967.

Outka, Gene; and John P. Reeder, Jr. (ed.), *Religion and Immortality.* Garden City, N.Y.: Anchor Books, 1973.

*Paley, William. "Natural Theology" in *The Works of William Paley.* Edinburgh: Brown & Nelson, 1825.

Pines, Shlomo. "Jewish Philosophy" in *Encyclopedia of Philosophy.* New York: Macmillan. 1967. Vol. 4, 261-276.

*Plato. "Phaedrus" in *Plato,* trans. Benjamin Jawette, ed. Robert Maynard Hutchins. Chicago: Encyclopedia Britannica Great Books of the Western World, 1952.

*Plotinus, "The Six Enneads" in *Plotinus,* trans. Stephen McKenna, ed. Robert Maynard Hutchins. Chicago: Encyclopedia Britannica Great Books of the Western World, 1952.

Reese, William L. *Dictionary of Philosophy and Religion: Eastern and Western Thought.* New Jersey: Humanities Press, 1980.

Rowe, William L; and William J. Wainwright (ed.), *Philosophy of Religion, Selected Readings.* San Francisco; Harcourt Brace Javanovich, 1973.

Scanlon, James P. "Alexander Nikolayevich Radishchev," in *Encyclopedia of Philosophy.* New York: Macmillan, 1967, Vol. 7, p. 63.

*Teilhard De Chardin, Pierre. *Christianity and Evolution.* New York: Harcourt Brace Javonovich, 1969.

*Thomas Aquinas, Saint. "Summa Theologica," in *Thomas Aquinas,* Vol, 1, trans. Fathers of the Dominican English Province, ed. Robert Maynard Hutchins. Chicago: Encyclopedia Britannica Great Books of the Western World, 1952.

Reischauer, August Karl. *The Naure and Truth of the Great Religions.* Vermont: Charles E. Tuttle, 1966.

Wienpahl, Paul. *The Radical Spinoza.* New York: New York U., 1979.

DICTIONARY

ANAXIMENES. He was the 6th Century Greek philosopher who believed that air was the basic substance of the universe and was the substance of the soul.

AEVITERNITY. According to Augustine and Aquinas, aeviternity is a state "between" time and eternity. Unlike time which has a beginning and an end, and eternity which has no beginning and no end, aeviternity has a beginning but no end. It is the state of the human soul. Aquinas also distinguishes aeviternity from time and eternity by explaining that eternity has no before and after; time has a before and after plus newness and oldness; aeviternity has a before and after but no newness and oldness.

ALBERT THE GREAT. Born around the year 1210 in Llauingen, Bavaria, Albert became a Dominican priest and lectured in theology at the University of Paris where one of his pupils was none other than Thomas Aquinas. Albert's published works are mainly in the sciences and in natural philosophy. English titles of his major works are: *Handbook of Doctrine Concerning Creatures, Commentary on the Four Books of Lombard's Sentences,* and *Handbook of Theology.* Albert was mainly an apologist. His works were an attempt to reconcile Christian ideas with pagan science. For two years beginning in 1260 he served as bishop of Ratisborn but his true interests were always science and philosophy, to which he quickly returned. He died in Cologne in 1280. He was canonized by the Church.

AQUINAS, THOMAS. An Italian philosopher and Doctor of the Church who lived from 1225 to 1274, Aquinas is one of the major saints of the Roman Catholic Church. He came from a wealthy family, was privileged to receive an excellent education, but to the chagrin of his family, particularly his mother, he joined the itinerant but respected Dominicans in 1244. Aquinas copied and expanded on many of the ideas of Aristotle. His most famous work is his *Summa Theologica* in which he gives his five proofs for the existence of God. The Catholic Church whole-heartedly endorses his teachings which touch upon just about every area of human activity.

ARCHETYPE.   By archetype is meant the original model from which all things of the same type are, in a general sense, copies. Today the word prototype is much more in use. From a strictly philosophical point of view, the term archetype really means "idea" more than anything else.

AUGUSTINE.   He was born in Tagaste in 354 and raised as a Christian. But he turned his back on Christianity about the time he began his studies in Carthage. Highly influenced later on by the teachings of St. Ambrose, Augustine eventually rejoined the Church, finally to become a priest then a bishop. He was both an apologist and a mystic as well as a philosopher. His writings greatly influenced Aquinas, according to some sources, and most of his works have been translated into English. He died in 430 while Bishop of Hippo when that town was besieged by the Vandals.

AVICENNA.   Born in the year 980, Avicenna was both a physician and philosopher. From the 10th Century until the beginning of the 16th, his was one of the most famous names in the field of medicine. His great work of the time as the *Canon of Medicine*. Avicenna was no less respected as a philosopher than he was as a physician. His metaphysical works draw a "picture" of God as the *Necessary Existent* who is, at one time, simple, eternal and the cause of all that exists. He believed that the human soul was created at the same time with the human body, as Aquinas later preached also. But Avicenna underscroed that the soul is in no way dependent upon the body for its own existence and that it is immortal. He lived the last years of his life as physician to the ruler of Isfahon and died in 1030.

BEING.   In philosophy, this term generally refers to what something is in principle rather than what it is in terms of its physical construction. Essentially, *being* is the unchanging quality of a thing.

BERKELEY, GEORGE (1865-1753).   He was the Irish philosopher who taught that matter only exists because mind recognizes it. Mind and soul are simply different names for the same thing. The soul is infinite, can never die, and is made of the same spiritual essence which ultimately defines the universe.

BOETHIUS, ANICIUS MANLIUS SERVINUS.   Boethius was a Roman philosopher and statesman who lived from 475-525. He was a consul and a minister to Theodoric, the king of the Ostrigoths. His relationship with Theodoric turned for the worse during a series of political evens which climaxed in charges of treason being brought against Boethius. The results were his being put into prison in Pavia, his sentencing without the opportunity of trial, and finally his execution. It was while he was imprisoned that he wrote his famous *De Consolatione Philosophiae* in both prose and in verse. The book is actually a dialogue between the writer himself and an entity which is Philosophy itself. *Philosophiae* was not Boethius' only work. He also wrote on religious and theological matters, on mathematics and music; and he did a number of translations of famous philosophical works.

BRUNO, GIORDANNO (1545-1600). He was a Dominican until the Church interpreted his teachings as being heretical. He subsequently left the order and continued to formulate his ideas. He believed the soul to be a monad consisting of the same substance which made up the universe. He was burned at the stake for his ideas, which the Church had justed to be against Catholic dogma.

CAJETAN, CARDINAL. Born Thomas de Vio in Gaeta, Italy in 1468, Cajetan became one of the more important theologians and philosophers of his time. Probably his most famous work is *Commentary on St. Thomas' Summa of Theology* in which he attempts to interpret the true meaning behind the ideas of Aquinas. In his own writings and arguments, however, he never tried to be quite as ambitious as Aquinas and often resorted to faith rather than logic in his explanations of the mysteries of creation, the idea of immortality, and the idea of God.

CITY OF GOD. This is one of the major works of St. Augustine. Like many Christians of his time, Augustine believed that the Roman Empire was, in fact, an eternal state. But in the year 410 the Visigoths moved on Rome and destroyed the city. This inspired Augustine, who was by this time already beginning to reevaluate his ideas about the empire, to develop and produce *City of God.* In this work, Augustine explains that it is wrong to see the empire in terms of any divine plan — or, for that matter, any society of man. As Augustine explains it, men must choose to live in the city of God or the city of man. But, he points out, only the first has its place in the divine scheme of things but the two cities must exist in parallel in the world in which we live. This is to say that each and every man and woman must learn to incorporate the values that are eternal in the city of God while they yet reside in the city of man. One might see this work as an important attempt to separate church and state in the minds of the Christians living during Augustine's time.

CONCERNING HUMAN UNDERSTANDING. One of John Locke's classic works, this text is the famed philosopher's investigation of knowledge and our ability to comprehend it. Locke believed that there is no possibility that man can ever understand the purpose of God, of life, of anything at all unless he is able to experience that knowledge through his senses. According to him, therefore, all our ideas have been acquired through our senses. With our rational abilities we can investigate the particular ideas that our senses relay to us; then we form generalizations about them. Thus, our ability to construct universal concepts is derived from the particular understandings we have first sensed, then contemplated. Every idea is born of experience.

CONTRIVANCE. By contrivance, and we come across this word often in teleological arguments, is meant the fabrication of some item, inorganic or organic. As teleologists explain it, wherever we can find signs of contrivance in the universe it must necessarily follow that there has been, or is, a contriver. Because this is true of mechanical objects which by their intricate designs show proof of purposeful and intellectual effort so must it be true of natural objects which are in themselves intricately designed for some specific purpose.

CORRUPTIBLE. By this term is meant *death* in the sense of final termination, in the sense of oblivion. Thus we say that the human body is corruptible because we know that it dies, that it ceases to be, that it decays and disappears forever. The soul, on the other hand, we say is incorruptible because it is immaterial, is essential and cannot be destroyed — or so some hope.

COSMOLOGY. This is the study, in both philosophy and science, of the universe, its cause and purpose. The term is employed here specifically in the philosophical sense in which it refers to the study of cause and effect to find the ultimate cause, that Prime Mover. In the cosmological arguments for God, for instance, philosophers look at cause and effect in nature to reason that there must indeed be a first and efficient cause which is not caused by any other, a first mover that is not moved by any other. Opponents to the cosmological argument for God counter that just because we cannot trace every cause and effect back to a first mover is no reason to assume there is a first mover; and if there is such a thing this does not mean it is God in the sense of that all powerful intellect we have come to conceive as being God.

"CRITIQUE OF PRACTICAL REASON."   One of Kant's classics, published about 1790. Here he continues to discuss the idea of moral imperatives but he makes clear that the pursuit of the necessary ends cannot be held above immediate moral duty. To Kant, every moral action has intrinsic value and can never be ignored. A translation of this work may be found in the Encyclopedia Britannica series *Great Books of the Western World.*

"CRITIQUE OF PURE REASON."   Probably Kant's greatest work, "Pure Reason" is his critical discussion of subjects such as pure and empirical knowledge; analytic and synthetic judgements; paralogisms of pure reason; the anatomy, ideal, cannon and history of pure reason. A translation of this work may be found in the Encyclopedia Britannica series *Great Books of the Western World.*

CYCLICAL RECURRENCE.   This is the idea that people and events which have occurred in cosmic history will occur over and over again, without fail, and in the same succession and detail as before.

DEATH.   In the sense in which the term is used throughout this text, death simply refers to the final corruption of the body but not to the final corruption of the personality or soul.

"DE CONSOLITIONE PHILOSOPHIAE."   This is the most famous work of Anicius Manlius Servernius Boethius (475-525); it was written while he was imprisoned in Pavia. The text is concerned mainly with the eternal nature of God and the aeviternity of things which God has brought into existence.

DEMOCRITUS (460-370 BC).   He was the Greek materialist who saw the universe as consisting of minute particles (atoms) which are indivisible, indestructible. They are so minute as to go undetected by any of our senses. The souls of men and women are like these atoms, which are freed to form again when the body which surrounds them dies.

DESCARTES, RENE. Rene Descartes (1596-1650) was a French philosopher and scientist who, as a young man, was fortunate enough to have received a Jesuit education. He served for a time in the army of Prince Maurice of Nassau, then at the age of 32 settled in Holland where he began a life dedicated to research and writing. He saw nature as being a very separate entity than that in which the human mind exists. That the mind does function within a physical form and in the realm of nature, according to Descartes, is only because this is God's design.

EMPEDOCLES (495 BC?-435 BC?). He was a Greek politician and philosopher who eventually found himself being exiled along with his followers. At one time the Greek people wanted to make him king but he had no interest in political dictatorship. Empedocles taught that the four elements — fire, earth, water and air — are indestructible, for they have always been in existence, and that matter itself, which is made up of these elements, is indestructible also.

"ENNEADS, THE." This is the title of Plotinus' philosophy, so named because each book consists of nine tractates. In the *First Ennead,* Plotinus discusses man, virtue, happiness and evil; in the second, the cosmos; in the third, fate, providence, time and eternity; in the fourth, the soul; in the fifth, the intellect.

EPICURUS (341-270 BC). He was the Greek philosopher who preached moderation and believed that the purpose of philosophy is to guide men and women to happiness. He saw the soul as being material in nature, its composition consisting of numerous atoms. But as the soul is material, it cannot be immortal.

"ESSAIS." Montaigne's works on the affairs of men and how they can best be handled. The essays in this collection are considered to be the greatest ever written. They were published in 1850.

ETERNAL. The word *eternal* has come to have a number of different meanings but in this text is generally meant to define something which has had no beginning and will have no end. Something eternal, then, is something which has no duration in either direction; that is, no duration into either the past or the future.

"ETHICS." This is Benedict De Spinoza's famous work in which he discussed God, the nature and origin of the mind, the nature and origin of affects, human bondage and human liberty, and the immortality of the mind.

EUCKEN, RUDOLF CHRISTOPH. He was a German philosopher. He received a Nobel prize in literature in 1908. Eucken believed that there is a supernatural thread that binds together all men and women. To Eucken, man's existence begins with his physical birth but his life transcends the physical. Born in 1846, Euckin died in 1926.

FECHNER, GUSTAV. He was a German philosopher who pioneered experimental psychology. Born in Prussia in 1801, Fechner was a professor of philosophy at the University of Leipsig. He believed that the universe we know is not natural in the true sense of the term, that is, not natural in substance. The universe is supernatural, as it exists fundamentally in the mind of God. It has become natural only because God had at some time decided to give it physical form. Fechner died in 1887.

EXISTENCE. It is particularly easy to identify those things which we can experience with our senses as existing. However, we cannot so easily determine whether or not things which are only knowable as mental concepts have real counterparts. For instance, we can know that cows exist, as Bertrand Russell once pointed out for us, because we know of at least one cow that is in existence. We see a cow and then we form a concept of just exactly what is a cow. We are sure that the concept is of something which is in existence because we have physical proof. In the case of God, however, the concept precedes our experiencing Him because he is very singular, so while we can develop a concept of Him we can never be sure that this concept is of something which indeed has existence.

FICINO, MARSILIO. Ficino (1433-1499) founded the Florentine Academy, held various positions in the Church and was a canon of the Florence Cathedral. Ficino saw that in all created things there were degrees of perfection with God rightfully at the top of the hierarchy. He also saw the soul as a very special creation which tied together the worlds of the natural and the supernatural.

HERACLITUS (535?-475 BC). He was the Greek philosopher who believed the only true reality to be the mind. He believed fire to be the basic substance of the universe and the human soul to be a special kind of fire.

IMMATERIAL. This term refers to those things which have no material form though they may in fact inhabit a material body. The soul is an example. We cannot sense it; it is not material in substance; and requires no physical union to continue its existence.

IMMORTAL. This term refers to that which has been brought into existence but will continue to exist for infinite time or beyond time. The soul of man is considered by many philosophers to be immortal though the body of man is mortal.

INCORRUPTIBLE. This term refers to that which, though its physical form may at anytime change or diminish or even corrupt, its essential nature can never be destroyed.

INFINITY. This term has a number of different meanings. In mathematics it defines that quantity which is beyond any that can be conceived. In geometry it represents unending distance. In philosophy the term also means these things but it also means existence without end.

IQBAL, MUHAMMED. He was an Islamic poet who was born Sialkot, Pakistan in 1877 and who died in 1938. He envisioned God as the ultimate Ego and man as a part of that Ego, yet distinct from it. Iqbal was a highly influential force on Muslim life in his time. In 1930 he served as the president of the Muslim League and in 1951, fourteen years after his death, the government of Pakistan established the Iqbal Academy which was committed to establishing new understanding of the ideas of this great poet.

JAMES, WILLIAM. James (1742-1910) was the son of Henry James, Sr., and the brother of the novelist Henry James. William's major work was *Principles of Psychology,* but it is by no means his only work, as he was a prolific writer. His very last work, *Some Problems of Philosophy: A Beginning of an Introduction to Philosophy,* was never completed but has been published.

KANT, IMMANUEL.   Kant was one of the most influential philosophers of his time, and among the most influential philosophers since his time. In 1781 he published his *Critique of Pure Reason* but it brought him little success with friends and colleagues. He later followed this work with *Critique of Practical Reason* and *Critique of Judgement* and these texts were well received and so much so that he won most of the following he had lost with *Pure Reason.* Kant remained a bachelor for his entire life, was a teacher by profession, and generally always in poor health. Born in 1724 in Konigsburg, East Prussia, he died in 1804.

LEIBNITZ, GOTFRIED WILHELM (1646-1716).   He was the German philosopher and mathematician who saw the universe as consisting of spiritual units of energy called monads. God is the greatest monad.

LOCKE, JOHN.   He was an English moral and political philosopher, well known for his *Essays Concerning Human Understanding* and other works. Locke (1632-1704) had a puritan upbringing, but a rather enlightened one. He grew up to be a firm supporter of religious tolerance. He favored the cosmological argument for the existence of God, accepted Scripture as being divinely inspired, and held that the human mind was incapable of discovering *all* the answers to God and His purpose for men and women.

MATERIAL.   By material is meant that which has physical body or can at least be recognized by one of the senses — as wind which can be felt and heard though not seen as well as animal forms which can be detected by all senses. Material things are seen as being corruptible, immaterial things incorruptible.

"METAPHYSICS."   This is the great work by Aristotle. It is divided into 14 parts (or books) in which he discusses among other things: philosophy, being, unity, eternalness and the first mover, immaterial substances.

MYERS, FREDERICK (1843-1901). He was an English psychical researcher also known for his essays and poetry. He believed that just as the world is governed by laws of science, so is the spirit world. He taught at Trinity College, Cambridge and helped found the Society for Psychical Research in 1882.

MILL, JOHN STUART. He was an English economist and philosopher who lived from 1806-1873. During his lifetime he became one of the most influential men in his fields. His written works are extensive. Among them are the following titles: *Principles of Political Economy, System of Logic, Subjection of Women, Civilization.* There is no known collection of his works to this date which contain all of his writings.

MONTAIGNE, MICHEL DE. Born in 1533 in Bordeaux, Montaigne grew up to become an essayist and philosopher. His essay *Apology For Raymond Seband,* in which he argues that religion should come from faith rather than reason, is purportedly his most famous work. Montaigne died in 1592.

MORAL ARGUMENT FOR THE EXISTENCE OF GOD. This is one of the four philosophical arguments for the existence of God. It was most notably put forth by Immanuel Kant and the argument is closely associated with his name. The argument holds that there are moral rules which seem to bind all men and women everywhere. These rules he interprets as "commands." Where there are moral commands, Kant reasons, there must be a moral commander.

MYTHOLOGY. Stories about supernatural events which are sometimes confused with sagas and legends that deal with characters and events which are within the realm of believability although greatly exaggerated. Myths, however, always deal with subjects of an extraordinary nature. Thus, the close association between religion and myth. Myth was almost always used in ancient times to account for phenomena that could not be explained naturally — phenomena such as stars and meteorites or fire or any event that was beyond the control or understanding of the civilization of the time.

NEWTON, ISAAC. Newton (1642-1727) was an English mathematician and physician. He met with unusual fame with the publication of his first book *Philosophiae Naturalis Principia Mathematica* which he had written mainly as a reply to queries from Edmund Halley about planetary movements. Newton also published works on history, theology, physics, optics and metaphysics.

NIETZCHE, FREDERICK (1844-1900). He was a German philosopher as well as poet. A man of continually poor health, he developed a rather pessimistic attitude about life. He was a moral skeptic and did not believe in God but he did believe in cyclical recurrence. He is claimed by some to have gone mad in his last year of life.

NIHILISM. This is a term very closely associated with the idea of atheism. In philosophy it is especially associated with one man: Frederick Nietzche. He, however, argued that nihilism and atheism did not necessarily go hand-in-hand. Nihilism is pessimism. Nihilist philosophers see no special meaning to life. They are moral skeptics. If they do acknowledge the possibility of God's existence, they argue that He has little interest in the affairs or happiness of the creatures He has brought into existence.

ONTOLOGY. Ontology forms a branch of metaphysics which deals with investigations designed to reveal the basic nature of *being* as well as the kinds of existence. One of the classical arguments for the existence of God is the ontological argument. It was most notably set down by St. Anselm (1033-1109), archbishop of Cantebury. It goes something like this: God is something of which nothing greater can be conceived. We may not at first admit that God actually exists but we must admit, at least, that the *idea of God* exists. But is this idea of a true being? Anselm says *yes,* otherwise we could conceive of something even greater — but, then, this would be a contradiction for our idea of God incorporates the idea that He is the greatest thing which exists. The ontological argument for the existence of God is still widely respected; however, it is by no means considered conclusive.

ORPHEUS. He was probably a mythical individual whose name and background appeared often in early Greek literature. As the stories go, he was a poet whose music was so beautiful that it calmed even the wild beasts. His wife died from the bite of a serpent and Orpheus went into Hades to find her and there so enthralled the gods with his music that they gave his wife (Eurydice) back to him. But there was one qualification they imposed: as he climbed from Hades back to earth, Orpheus must never look upon his wife. He failed the condition, however, and Eurydice was again taken from him.

PALEY, WILLIAM. He was an English theologian and philosopher, most remembered for his teleological argument in *Natural Theology,* which he had published in 1802. Paley was born in 1743, was ordained in 1767 and became a lecturer in moral philosophy at Christ's College in Cambridge. His first extensive work was *Principles of Moral and Political Philosophy* in 1785. On religious matters he was mainly an apologist. Paley was what might be considered an "easy" philosopher in that he presented or defended his ideas in, what was for his time, simple but effective prose. He died in 1805.

PESSIMISM.   See "nihilism."

PHILO JUDAEUS.   Born about 20 BC, Philo is generally referred to as an Alexandrian Jewish philosopher. His ideas and writings had a notable influence on both Jewish and Christian theologians. Not all of his works have been found but for the most part Philo was influenced to a very great extent by Plato. Philo saw the law of the Old Testament as being the basis for all philosophy, supported the cosmological argument for the existence of God and interpreted God to be not merely the Prime Mover but also the creator of all that exists.

PIERCE, CHARLES SANDERS.   He was an American physicist and philosopher who was born in Cambridge, Massachusetts in 1839. He worked as an astromoner, physicist and teacher. Though married twice, Pierce never had any children. He was, basically, a student of Kant's works but he went on to develop his own systems of logic. He died in 1914.

PLATO.   He was the famous Greek philosopher who lived sometime between 427 and 347 BC. He became a pupil and trusted friend of Socrates. He was the founder of a school called the Academy where he preoccupied himself with teaching both mathematics and philosophy. His writings are extensive for an ancient and they are, as well, highly influential. He was not a man very enthralled with life as it is generally lived by men and women and preferred a life of contemplation. He believed in the immortality of the soul and offered ontological, cosmological and teleological arguments for the existence of God.

PLOTINUS.   He was a neoplatonist philosopher who lived from 205 to 270 AD. He was an Egyptian of Roman descent. His theories were basically the same as that of Plato. He joined the military expedition of Emperor Gorian III with the sole intention of learning what he could about Indian and Persian philosophy. Much of what we know about Plotinus we owe to his pupil and biographer, Porphyry.

PRINCIPLE. In the sense in which the term has been used in this text, it has meant the primary source, as the soul would be the principle of the man or woman and God would be the principle of life.

PRINGLE-PATTISON, ANDREW SETH. He was a Scottish philosopher who held the chair of logic and metaphysics at the University of S. Andrew. Seth (1856-1934) took on the name Pringle-Pattison to meet the conditions set down in a will which would entitled him to a valued inheritance. Seth believed there were limits to philosophy. It could bring men to finding many answers but certainly not all of them. He believed in a personal immortality but one that was conditional depending upon the judgement of God.

PSYCHE. This word is basically a synonym for mind, intellect or soul. Philosophical debate will continue on whether the psyche is separate from the body, is a part of the body, is host to the body (that is, the body is a part of *it*), or even exists at all.

PYTHOGORAS. He was a Greek philosopher. He is somewhat of a mystery to historians as there is little available on his personal life. We do know however that he was born in 582 and died in 507 BC. His followers were quite naturally referred to as Pythogorians and they were greatly influenced by the ideas attributed to that possibly mythical character, Orpheus. But the Pythogorians were mathematicians as well as philosophers and in their pursuit of knowledge wound up contradicting the public and religious practices of their time. Much of what Pythogoras' personal observations and reflections may have been must be drawn from the teachings of his followers. Pythogoras evidently believed that all the universe could be described in purely mathematical terms. He, or his followers, were the first to realize that the Earth was no more than a planet. Pythogoras believed in the superiority of the psyche and saw all of life as a means to its education.

RADISHCHEV, ALEXANDER NIKOLAYEVICH. He was a Russian philosopher who lived from 1749 to 1802. He was born in Moscow and studied at the University of Leipsig. He met with great success in both the civilian and military positions he held in life. When he was 41 years old he published his famous *A Journey from St. Petersburg to Moscow* and was subsequently exiled to Siberia by Catherine the Great. He saw experience as the only means by which knowledge could be learned and that all we sense is fundamentally symbolic and while we are able to identify the things we observe by various names, their true identity and meaning are beyond our intellectual grasp.

RUSSELL, BERTRAND. He was a British philosopher and mathematician. Russell (1872-1970) had an extremely colorful and diversified career. He was a determined pacifist, supporter of women's rights, candidate for public office, teacher and social critic. He did not believe in the immortality of the soul. Some of his major works include: *Principles of Mathematics, Why I Am Not a Christian, the Wisdom of the West.*

SCHOPENHAUER, ARTHUR. He was a German philosopher who lived from 1888 to 1960. His father died when he was still in his teens and his relationship with his mother, a novelist, were always strained. His philosophy is one of pessimism and while this philosophy is greatly studied and discussed, it is rarely supported.

SOCRATES. He was an Athenian philosopher who lived from 469-399 BC. Socrates put nothing in writing. What we know of his ideas comes to us from the works of his student, and good friend, Plato. Socrates saw his life as one meant to be dedicated to the religious education of his fellow men. In 399 he was charged with corrupting the youth, particularly by leading them away from worship of the Greek gods. Ths charge was contrived but legally effective. Socrates was condemned to death. His trial and death are recorded in various works by Plato: *Apology, Crito, Phaedo.*

SOUL. See *PSYCHE.*

SPINOZA, BARUCH. He was a Dutch philosopher who lived from 1632-1677. He was educated as an orthodox Jew but his studies in Latin brought him into contact with the ideas of many of the great philosophers. He was a lens grinder by trade but mainly worked to support his writings on philosophy. He was at one time offered a professorship at Heidelberg but he preferred his humble occupation that left him the time and seclusion needed to develop his ideas on paper. He is most remembered for his *Ethics,* published ten years after his death.

TEILHARD DE CHARDIN, PIERRE. He was a French Jesuit who became renowned for his geological and paleontological research. He lived from 1881 until 1955. Some of his theological writings were suppressed by the Catholic Church but they were finally published after his death. Teilhard attempted to show that there was some consistency between the findings of science and the ideas of religion.

TELEOLOGY. Not to be confused with the word *THEOLOGY,* teleology is the study of proofs of design, and its purpose of that design, in nature.

VIVES, JUAN LUIS (1492-1510). He was the Spanish humanist philosopher who believed that the soul was the essential driving force in each man and woman.

Index